You're the
Daddy

From nappy mess to happiness in one year

The art of being a great dad

You're the
Daddy

From nappy mess to happiness in one year
The art of being a great dad

Stephen **Giles**

Editors: **Richard Craze**, **Roni Jay**

new tricks for old dogs

Published by White Ladder Press Ltd
Great Ambrook, Near Ipplepen, Devon TQ12 5UL
01803 813343
www.whiteladderpress.com

First published in Great Britain in 2006

10 9 8 7 6 5 4 3 2

ISBN 1 905410 00 X
ISBN 978 1 905410 00 2

British Library Cataloguing in Publication Data
A CIP record for this book can be obtained from the British Library.

Designed and typeset by Julie Martin Ltd
Cover design by Julie Martin Ltd
Cover photograph by Jonathon Bosley
Cover models Charlie Benns and Peter Baker
Printed and bound by TJ International Ltd, Padstow, Cornwall

White Ladder Press
Great Ambrook, Near Ipplepen, Devon TQ12 5UL
01803 813343
www.whiteladderpress.com

To our mums –
who had their own battles

Acknowledgements

Thanks as ever to Lindsay and the boy for putting up with me. I'm indebted to David Burke and Steve Fountain for their wise criticism, to the surveyed fathers for more thought provoking and surprising insights, and to Roni and Rich at White Ladder for everything else.

Contents

Information Panels

Introduction

Maybe you're about to become a father for the first time, maybe your baby has already arrived, or you're on to the second, third or fourth child. Or maybe you're just browsing in a bookshop to get out of doing the shopping. Whichever applies, one thing is true – this book will help.

This book will help because becoming a dad isn't a simple process – even if you've done it before – nor is it something that comes naturally to most of us. This book will help because there's a whole minefield of new experience out there waiting for you – new stresses, relationship challenges, fears and compromises. As with pregnancy, it's your partner who has the support network and advice on tap. You have instinct, common sense and not a lot else. But now you have this book – a guide and a fellow traveller to help you negotiate a safe path to happiness.

Most dads-to-be that I've met say they want to be hands-on when the baby arrives. It's a phrase that can mean many things – from dealing with all the nappies and night-time feeds to occasionally bouncing the kid on one knee while watching the football. But generally it suggests a desire to play an important role in the early stages of this new life.

It's an incredible role to play, and each time it is unique and special. But we all come up against the same milestones, the same prejudices and fears. The difference is in the way we handle them – the more prepared we are, the better equipped we'll be to respond in the best way possible.

This book is the frank and sometimes frustrated journal I kept during my first year as a father – over that time I sampled every style of fatherhood, from the traditional full time working role to acting as principal carer for our baby via every possible combination in between. This journal is interlaced with the hints, tips and advice I received at the time and after the events. The book also draws heavily on the experiences of other new fathers – my thanks to them once again for agreeing to be surveyed and helping to create a truly broad picture of new fatherhood.

There is a very deliberate structure to this book, which reflects one of the best pieces of advice I've been given about fatherhood – by a friend who's been there and done it three times over. Fatherhood, said my mate, is all about stages. Initially it can feel like you're only able to think about the next day, but this soon becomes the next week or the next month as life gradually returns to normal. So the first chapter focuses on the first days, the second on the first week, the third on the first six weeks and so on to one year and beyond. At each stage the art of being a great dad becomes easier, clearer and more rewarding until you have built the most incredible relationship.

In all my conversations and experiences of fatherhood, I've found that one essential ingredient for success is confidence. It's hard to get this without experience and it's downright impossible without encouragement, support and enthusiasm. This book aims to provide all three.

So welcome to a new world. It's strange and sometimes unfriendly and it will occasionally leave you feeling disorientated and wistful for your uncomplicated past life. But I guarantee that, given the chance, you'll find incredible highs and new talents you'd never imagined.

So, life begins. Again.

Chapter One
Baby meets Dad

Last night I became a dad. From what I recall of 11.04pm – the exact time of my son's arrival – there were no trumpets or angels, not even much wailing or gnashing of teeth. I remember thinking it was just after time at the bar. Time to sober up.

I didn't feel very sober, but I was a long way from the pub. I was in an operating theatre, struggling to get my head around the incredible events of the previous few hours. It all started when my wife Lindsay was rendered virtually immobile due to the pelvic pain that dogged her pregnancy. She was enduring this pain and the agony of contractions for what seemed like an eternity, before a decision was taken to give her an emergency caesarean section.

Within minutes this was done, our son was presented to us and I was sent into a side room while the medical staff stitched up my battered and embattled wife. Then the boy was lowered into my arms for his first man to man cuddle. One heavy lidded eye peered suspiciously at the fluorescent outside world, the other remained tightly shut, intent on sneaking a bit more sleep. Five minutes old and just like his dad.

Eventually, Lindsay and the boy were packed off for the ward – I stayed with them until they were settled and then I was asked to leave. I got home around 1am, bleary eyed and disorientated but still wide awake. Our cold, dark house was a sudden and stark contrast to the blazing heat and bright lights of the hospital. I felt dizzy, nauseated and mentally exhausted. Which made it the perfect time to ring the family.

Hi, it's Stephen. *A very tired 'hello'.* Yeah, just ringing to, em....*Excited 'yes'.* To tell you....*Impatient 'yes'.* That Lindsay has had, that we've, rather, had....*Sound of teeth grinding, followed by frustrated 'yes'.* A boyby. Baby. A baby boy.

A sigh from me as they paused, then the champagne cork of their congratulations burst out, followed by the bubbles of a million questions about weight, height, name and voting preference. I recalled what little I could and pleaded ignorance of the finer details – including his name, which still hadn't been decided. I rang my best mate and told him that I didn't have a clue what I was doing. He seemed to understand.

After that I drank some liquid, ate some solids, considered placing all the detergent bottles on a high shelf and rounding off the corners on the dining table, decided against, went to stand in the nursery for a while then headed off to bed with Five-Minute Tales. I was asleep within four.

The final thing Lindsay said to me last night was that I should have a lie-in and take my time getting to the hospital. Tempting though this was, I didn't want to sleep through my son's first morning in the world, so I set an alarm. It turned out to be totally unnecessary as the cat woke me at six, scratching at the bedroom door. She needed to go outside, and though she has a perfectly good, and permanently open, window for this purpose, she always likes to make a grand exit through the front door in the mornings.

The dogs, currently vacationing at Hotel Parents-in-law, have similarly irritating quirks. My life is spent satisfying the strange whims of my dependents. Now there's another – and though we've only just been introduced I know I'll be jumping through hoops to keep him happy for years.

This morning was bright and cold, the kind of weather that would make you feel alive even if you hadn't just been through an extraordinary life changing experience. I went to the shop to get some drinks and magazines for Lindsay and just couldn't keep the huge, conspiratorial grin off my face. I was desperate for someone I knew to show up so I could babble incomprehensibly about our new arrival.

But they didn't, and though it was tempting to bend the captive ear of the poor woman behind the shop counter, I kept it all in until I got to the hospital. I arrived about three minutes after the start of visiting hours and headed straight for the side ward where they'd wheeled Lindsay and the boy last night. They'd been the sole inmates then, and I hoped they still were – I wanted today to be about us as a family.

Don't ask the family
Learning the ropes in privacy

The one part of fatherhood I get almost evangelical about is the few hours or couple of days spent together in the hospital after the birth.

It's so important to put your new family first. Friends, relations and well-wishers are wonderful people to have around and they add tremendously to the experience, but unless they are blessed with the patience and tact of saints they will muscle in on bonding time that should be yours and yours alone. The only way we could guarantee this was to ban all family and friends from the hospital – and it's something I heartily recommend. It doesn't mean you have to exclude the family altogether, as they can play an important (and absorbing) part looking after pets, houses or other children while you're focused on the new arrival.

It also depends on individual circumstances – if your partner is to stay in hospital for a week that's a long time to keep new grandparents away, if she's out within hours then you might want to allow family to visit during your brief time in hospital, then insist on a couple of days' privacy when she gets out. But whether you're at home or on the ward, I recommend you 'ring-fence' some time to learn all the tricks of the trade in splendid isolation.

I strode briskly down the corridor, full of pride and nervous anticipation. I peered into side wards where pasty faced new mothers sat up in bed, surrounded by semicircles of family and friends passing round babies like fire buckets. The beds were decked with balloons, bedside tables groaned under the weight of cellophane wrapped bouquets. Eternity rings and lockets glinted in the light. Teddy bears stared impassively at me as I passed. I looked down at my carrier bag – three bottles of water for the price of two, a Radio Times to replace the out of date copy I sent Lindsay in with, a newspaper and two bars of chocolate, both of which I'd hoped to eat while she was distracted. It was just possible I'd made my first huge mistake as a father.

When I got to the ward, they were still alone. This was great, as it meant we had uninterrupted family time and eased the likelihood of balloon envy. Anyway, Lindsay has all the gifts she wants – our boy and a gradual, miraculous easing of the joint pain that's kept her on crutches for weeks. This morning she was serene, tired and very happy. The boy was sleeping peacefully in a plastic fish tank next to the bed. I was a bundle of nerves.

We sat and whispered for a while. The most pressing topic was his name. We still hadn't decided, though we'd ruled out many using the tried and tested method of 'did you hate someone at school with that name'? My list ran into hundreds, with the notable exception of Oliver. Lindsay agreed. After weeks of negotiation, arbitration and lobbying it was as simple as that.

Oliver slept on, unaware that we'd finally reached a significant decision. Lindsay confessed that she'd had a sleepless night, due in part to Oliver's occasional waking periods, but also to the sheer excitement and wonderment of having him alongside her. I said she should have a nap, that I'd watch Oliver if he woke. She smiled, turned her back to me and was snoring gently in an instant. Bugger. What if he did wake? What was I going to do then?

The cogs in my brain must be louder than I realise, because within a few minutes he was stirring. He didn't cry, it was more of a vaguely feline moan, but it was enough to prompt his mother to sit bolt upright in bed, shaken from her sleep. I'd barely left the chair and she was halfway to his tank. She stopped, paused and looked at me sheepishly.

"Go on," she said. "You go."

So I picked him up. Though it wasn't the first time I'd held him, I was almost shaking with nerves. I wanted to get it right, to show Lindsay that I knew what I was doing. I put one hand under his head and one under his bottom, then realised I was holding him at arms' length and could do nothing about it except put him back down or stay like that forever. I whimpered, and Lindsay scooped him gently from my inert grasp, backed me into the chair, indicated that I should crook my arm to make a rest for his head and shoulders and laid him down on my lap. Sitting was infinitely better than standing – I felt much more in control. Oliver peered at me with the same justifiable suspicion that he'd shown last night and then went back to sleep.

I've always laughed at the ludicrous statements new parents come out with, especially the arrogant assertion that their offspring have perfect fingers, toes, mouths, noses etc. Such comments appear even more extraordinary now, given that no other child could possibly achieve the perfection of Oliver's fingers, toes, mouth, nose, ears, legs, arms, body and head. And did I mention his beautiful eyes? Even his hair, dark and matted with unidentified gunk last night, is now cleaned to the kind of straw blond that has a certain greatness about it. I sat and marvelled at this supreme being as he huffed and puffed and wriggled, doubtless wondering why he wasn't lying in his cosy fish tank.

Within a few minutes he was back in the tank, in a deep sleep. Lindsay was snoozing again and I was reading the newspaper as quietly as possible. Family life had begun.

A midwife came into the room and rustled up to the bed – they must give them standard issue newspaper knickers. She leaned across Lindsay and said "Is she sleeping?" in the kind of measured stage whisper that would have reached the back row of the Coliseum at feeding time.

"Not any more, you clumsy, foghorn voiced idiot," I would have said, given half the chance. But Lindsay cut me off, springing up again like a jack-in-the-box.

"Thought you'd like a shower," the midwife said.

"Not as much as she'd like some rest," I spat, triumphantly. So what if they'd already left the room by then, I made my point. Lindsay, walking unaided, albeit tentatively, looked back at me from the doorway and smiled. I smiled back and nodded confidently. It was a nod that said 'take your time, have fun – and relax, all will be well'. How wrong can one nod be?

Two or three minutes passed, just long enough for Lindsay to get out of screaming range, then the first tremor hit. It was almost nothing – if the ward had been busy it might have gone unheard, but in the silence it rang out like a gunshot. Oliver shifted and started to moan. I poked my head into the tank. It hadn't sounded good and it didn't smell too great either. Using the latest keyhole surgery techniques I undid the microscopic poppers on his sleep suit, then repeated the process on his body suit. It was like pass the parcel played in hell – the closer I got to the prize, the more I wanted the music to stop so I could offload the problem. But no-one was in sight.

I'd reached the nappy. Disposable nappies, though arguably bad for the environment, have one fantastic feature – they generally have a cartoon of frolicking, sporty creatures on the front. This gives the clueless father – i.e. me - a chance to get the nappy the right way round without humiliating him with the words 'front' and 'back' stamped somewhere prominent.

I deduced that an uncomfortable, full nappy would be a horrible thing to stay in for any length of time, so I whipped it straight off. To my surprise it contained a black, sticky tar-like mess that was now all over Oliver, his clothes and his bed sheet. His cool eyes found my panicked gaze. I could tell he was contemplating his first word.

I ran across the ward with the little tin tray that the midwife gave us for nappy changes, filled it at the tap and ran back. In the meantime, liberated by the freedom of his private parts, he'd peed all over himself too. I took off his sodden clothes and laid him back down on a clean corner of the tank. I had to fill another tin tray with washing water. Back I went.

By this stage Oliver was, with total justification, upset. I wasn't exactly whistling chirpily either. Keeping up a faint soundtrack of 'shit, shit, shit, shit, shit', I dabbed feebly at his nether regions, cleaned him up and somehow swathed him in a nappy. After a desperate hunt through his bag, I found replacement clothes and wrestled them onto him. By the time I'd picked him up, cuddled him and stopped his crying our corner of the ward resembled a landfill site that had really let itself go. I stuck a towel in his cot, put him back in, tidied up and then, as if on cue, Lindsay wandered slowly back onto the ward.

"Alright?" she said. I just nodded.

A little while later a midwife came to show us how to bath Oliver and change his nappy. I'm sure she wondered why I kept giving little hollow laughs at her advice. But I also made sure I was listening very carefully.

Oh. My. God.
A short introduction to the nappy

It doesn't matter what the classes and books tell you, there's no substitute for experience when it comes to baby care. It's impossible to recreate the art of putting a nappy on a screaming child without using complex animatronics, so your best bet is to wait until you're presented with a real baby before you try.

However, that doesn't mean you're on your own – the midwives and auxiliary nurses on the maternity wing are on hand to offer basic advice on baby care and it doesn't reflect badly on you if you feel you need it, because we all do.

Depending on how arduous your partner's labour was and how long you can tolerate relatives in your house, there will almost certainly come a time in the next few days when you have to roll up your sleeves and change a nappy, or wash and dress the baby.

There are two essentials to remember – be prepared and don't panic. Before you start any given task, ensure you have all the necessary tools to hand – nappy, nappy bags, wipes or cotton wool and water, towel, clothes etc. You can't leave a baby, even a newborn, perched on a changing table while you go off hunting for kit. As a general rule, men tend to react to a given problem (i.e. dirty nappy) by remedying that problem (i.e. taking it off straight away) which can sometimes make matters worse. Be calm, methodical and businesslike. It's a matter of trust, if you can make the baby believe you are in control, then all will be well.

After a morning of non-stop excitement, this afternoon has been a gentle process of getting used to each other. We took a lengthy family stroll all the way to the TV room; we rang Lindsay's parents. We went back to the TV room and watched the rugby for a while. In spite of my excitement at being a proud dad I was starting to flag. The emotions that kept me going throughout yesterday's marathon session have virtually shut me down today. By teatime all I could think of was a comfy sofa, football on the TV and extended phone calls to family and friends to boast about Oliver.

Lindsay said she didn't mind me going – I suspect she's looking forward to a few hours with him on her own again. She's been brilliant today – hands-off, patient, tolerant – all the things I've needed to get confident handling Oliver. While a small part of me feels guilty for not allowing friends and family into the hospital, I also know if we'd allowed them to take over this practice session, I wouldn't have stood a chance.

However great it's been, time in the hospital doesn't remotely compare to time at home, and I can't wait for them to be discharged. The midwife thought it might be possible for them to come home tomorrow, which would be great, but I'm worried about Lindsay leaving hospital before she's ready, then ending up flat on her back for a month.

The original plan was for her to transfer to a cottage hospital run by midwives, where she could convalesce and bond with Oliver. But a few days of cranked up heat, crazy inmates and inedible food has changed our thinking dramatically.

Care in the community
Extending your partner's time in hospital

Convalescent hospitals managed by midwives are a great stepping stone if your partner's had a tough time during labour – and they offer a lot more baby care support. It's a more intimate and focused setting than a general hospital. On the downside they can leave you feeling pretty detached from the first few days of parenthood, and they may insist that friends and relatives stay away for the whole time.

In essence it's got to be your partner's choice – you may want her home out of a genuine desire to care for her and the baby, or just because you've run out of food and can't operate the tin opener. Bearing in mind the strain she's just been under, don't begrudge her the chance to take it easy if she wants to – there will be precious little time for rest at home.

If your partner's had a caesarean section there are some additional factors to bear in mind – she will be unable to lift heavy objects and may even struggle to lift or carry the baby. She won't be able to drive for six weeks. Under these circumstances, it's only really fair to bring her home if you're willing and able to take on the lion's share of work for the first month or more – and that's not likely to be practical. A preferable option after caesarean might be to entrust your partner's care to the convalescent hospital for the first week, then take your two weeks' paternity leave. That gives her three weeks to get more mobile and eases the stress on you.

The only part of the plan that isn't geared up for their triumphant return seems to be our house. It feels cold and harsh – the tiles on the floor are hazards in waiting, the fireplace is a potential nightmare and the stairs – well, don't even get me started on the stairs. For some reason I feel ultimately responsible for ensuring safety in the house. Everything has to be right but it patently won't be, not unless I can summon the energy to pad every surface and remove every danger. And, as I can't even summon the energy to shout at the inept footballers on the TV, it ain't going to happen. Babies are tough, babies are resourceful, babies are survival experts. That's right, keep repeating it, you lazy bastard.

Padded cell anyone?
Preparing your home for the baby

This is another area where the dual mantra of 'be prepared' and 'don't panic' holds true. There's no point 'baby proofing' the whole house, as junior won't be up and about for months.

You can, however, make some basic provisions for the return from hospital. Temperature is a big thing for newborns – as they aren't really adept at controlling their own. Make sure the rooms you're using for the baby have a decent ambient heat of around 18-21 degrees C.

If you've bought a cot or crib don't necessarily expect to use it straight away. Imagine you're a baby, wrenched from the cosiness of the womb – you're bound to be happier in confined spaces, so a padded Moses basket is a good first step. Move up to the crib or cot in a few weeks when the world doesn't seem like such a daunting place. There needs to be a safe, level place for this in the bedroom, the nursery and probably the lounge because the baby won't always go to sleep where you want it to.

With the exception of nappies, clothes and the car seat, you don't really need anything else right now, though that won't stop some well meaning friend buying your day old child a 4x4 quad bike. If friends and family are pestering you for gift ideas and you're struggling to fend them off, go for the failsafe option of plain bodysuits and sleepsuits – you can never have too many of these, and they'll save you from having to do endless washing.

• • •

The midwives weren't certain Lindsay would be signed off today, but we stated our intent clearly – all packed and ready to go by about 11am. That's made the day long and frustrating, because we've had to wait for the paediatrician to come and have a poke at Oliver to check that he's doing ok, and then another wait for Lindsay to be signed off. Yet again, they didn't get much sleep last night, mainly because of the presence of a loud, drunken woman on the ward – and I thought consultants only worked regular hours – so Lindsay's especially tired and fed up with the hospital.

But shortly after watching Lindsay do battle with another inedible lunch I was given the nod and got the chance to settle Oliver into his car seat, ready for the off. He looked so small and vulnerable in it that I immediately began to question the logic of placing him in or near a car driven by me. Far safer for Oliver and Lindsay to walk the five miles or so home. Sadly, she didn't see things the same way, so we went for the car option.

We said brief goodbyes to the midwives and scurried off, feeling like con-artists who've just stolen a priceless masterpiece. I got to carry Oliver in his seat, facing out so that the general public could catch their first glimpse of the prodigal son. Astonishingly, there were no swarms of adoring well-wishers swelling against crash barriers and no photographers on step ladders. In fact there was no-one at all – which only increased the feeling that we were stealing this fragile baby from under the noses of the authorities.

Safely installed in the car, I made a slow getaway. All I needed was the canvas flat cap and the tartan rug on my parcel shelf and I'd have been the consummate Sunday driver. I mirrored, signalled and manoeuvred with a care that hasn't been seen since my driving test. I finally found fourth gear on the dual carriageway, while waving to the elderly cyclist shaking his fist at me as he overtook. My driving may have been cautious, but I was overwhelmed by the sense of self-righteousness that accompanies transit of a precious cargo. I finally understand the mentality behind 'baby on board' stickers.

That still doesn't mean I want one.

As we pulled up outside the house I saw a familiar car parked next door. It was our former neighbours, who moved out a couple of weeks ago. New parents themselves of about six weeks standing, they'd popped over to pick up their mail. As we were unpacking the car, they came round to see us and coo over Oliver.

"He's gorgeous," they said. And I'm fairly sure I detected a significant degree of envy.

"Yes," I felt like saying, "but I'm sure your child will still make some sort of contribution in Oliver's new world order." But actually, I just grinned stupidly. I still feel guilty for extracting the poor boy from the safety of a hospital and totally bemused that someone so hopelessly flawed could help to produce such a beautiful child.

"Aren't you clever?"
Competitive Dad Syndrome – Stage One

This was the first time I displayed the symptoms of CDS – Competitive Dad Syndrome – a particularly ruthless illness of the mind that can affect any new father. It's hard to avoid, but there are ways – never use a video camera around your child, never involve your child in a sporting event, never dress your child in your favourite team's colours, never take your child to a public play park, or indeed any sort of public place.

As I've been guilty of all the above, I'm not well placed to advise on avoiding CDS, but I can offer some tips on moderating your behaviour around others. Rule one – introductions. When you introduce your baby to other people, they will almost certainly come out with 'Oh, he/she's beautiful'. If they're a new parent themselves (and they do tend to gravitate towards you) you should be aware that they're expecting a reciprocal compliment.

Sometimes this can be tough, forcing you to reach deep into the recesses of your vocabulary to find a polite way to describe the gargoyle writhing in their pram, but you must always say something, even if it's a distraction technique like 'he gets it from his mother', or 'look out for that bus'.

It's a British national characteristic to despise success that's easily worn, so if you want to keep the sympathy of well-wishers you'll add in something about how tough night-times are, or how he may look like an angel but he can be a demon. Try not to go too far the other way and let this turn into an anguished monologue.

In short, be confident of your child's beauty and talent and don't rely on second hand praise to validate you as a parent. I know that seems tough right now – but don't worry, we'll be coming back to it.

When we'd been to see our neighbours a week after their little girl was born, she was sleeping 12 hours a night and they were relaxed, confident and assured. It gave me so much confidence that I would cope with our own child. But now they are shadows of their former selves – she's stopped sleeping well and they're in a permanent trance. I don't know which version is our future, but I know which I'd rather.

We got Oliver inside, laid him down in his little carrycot and made ourselves a cup of tea. We sat and watched him for a while in silent wonder. Then I put the TV on.

This afternoon and evening have been dominated by a series of small tasks that have taken hours of planning, lengthy execution and an eternity of clearing up. We've managed to get the nappy change down to something manageable – around half an hour – but it still resembles a manual dexterity task from The Krypton Factor.

Washing the baby is even more of a juggling act and feeding is a slow and frustrating process for mother and son. He's not taking well to the breast, so he's getting some expressed milk too. Everything seems so huge – the clothes we've bought for him, his bed, his pram. It's all too soon, he's not done yet and he needs to go back in for a few months.

A giant leap for man
Playing a part from the start

The first few hours at home won't shape your parenting for ever, but they might set the pattern for the next couple of weeks. You've got a balancing act on your hands – now is a good time to perfect key baby care techniques, but you've also got to be mindful that you're not stepping between mother and child. Lindsay confessed later that she wanted to keep Oliver to herself as much as possible over the first couple of days, which is totally understandable, though not necessarily logical.

Try to be a part of everything in the first few hours at home because, however you plan to divide the childcare in the future, this time is about bonding, and both parents deserve an equal opportunity. Your partner is likely to be emotional, so tact is in order, but she'll also be physically exhausted, which is where you can help out and take your chance for quality time with the baby. So dive in at the deep end – the longer you wait to get involved, the harder it will be.

Eventually the time came to settle him down in his massive crib. We put a teddy in with him for company and sang him a song. He went off like a dream. It couldn't have been easier. But, by the time we'd got downstairs and finished congratulating each other, the hammering started – our new neighbour attempting a spot of DIY at 10pm on a Sunday. Oliver woke and started to cry, Lindsay screamed in frustration. I clenched my fists and went to introduce myself.

I'm not an angry person, and I did manage to keep a lid on my obvious fury. But I don't think we'll be holidaying together for a while. The hammering duly stopped and I returned, breathing deeply.

Oliver hasn't been so easy to quieten. He's found every excuse under the moon to stay awake all night. Our neighbour drove off about midnight – either to find somewhere quiet to sleep or to fetch his big brother with an even bigger hammer.

We've bravely attempted to sit with Oliver in shifts, but I can't sleep knowing Lindsay's stuck with an inconsolable child, and she feels the same. When all those knowing, cynical parents tell you that your baby's cries cut through you like a knife they're not kidding. It's impossible to ignore, and heartbreaking to hear.

At one stage I took him downstairs to give Lindsay a break and sat him in the swing that we bought him on a friend's recommendation. I started it rocking and playing its merry tune. This pushed Oliver to a new and hitherto unimagined level of misery. So he came out again and I cuddled him and sang to him and danced around the room until my feet were sore and my head was throbbing.

Scream test
How to survive the first night

In order to ensure that the planet stays populated, no-one tells you quite how awful it is to spend a night awake with your screaming child – which you'll probably be doing more in the first couple of weeks of fatherhood than at any other time.

It's almost impossible to convey the particular combination of anguish, frustration, guilt and regret that overwhelmed me on that first night – and to a lesser extent on many subsequent nights over the first few weeks. The worst part was feeling totally unable to console Oliver – I was genuinely frightened that we'd created this new life and had no understanding of it, that he was going to be miserable for ever and we weren't going to help.

Everyone's experience is different and most people find a way to cope in the end. The only hope I can offer while you're watching the Open University with the sound off in the wee small hours is that everything you experience with babies is a phase, good or bad. Whatever's going wrong will ultimately mend, whatever's going right will ultimately break. I don't know whether that's reassuring, but it makes perfect sense in the middle of the night.

As 4am approached, I laid down with him on the spare bed in his nursery – our most brilliant idea. He was exhausted, cuddling into my crooked arm and fighting for a comfortable space to doze off. Sleep was impossible for me, I kept worrying that he would fall out of bed or that I'd roll over onto him. As the new day started to lighten the fringes of the curtain, the worst thought in my mind was that this is how life will be from now. The way I feel is never going to change, I'm simply going to get used to it. It's just possible that we have made a truly terrible mistake.

Chapter Two
Baby meets family

There have been a few occasions in life when I've stayed awake all night – mainly when we've been going on holiday, and we're booked on an insanely early flight. By the time the night has passed I'm generally in a trance, an empty shell heading for the hotel and immediate collapse. Today is the first time in my life I've been through an all-nighter and still had to get up to face a long line of chores – and the inaugural visit of the new grandparents.

I started with the basics. As people were coming to visit, clothes were in order. Therefore it was necessary to get dressed. But this meant finding clothes and co-ordinating legs and arms. Too much to handle first off.

I went to the toilet, fortunately remembering to make it all the way to the bathroom first. Buoyed by this significant achievement I attempted the stairs. Another success. Arriving in the lounge like a triumphant explorer fresh back from the polar region, I noticed Lindsay had fed, changed, washed and clothed Oliver. I realised she must have secretly got some sleep while I wasn't looking. I resolved to hold this against her for all eternity. And then I found myself in the cupboard under the stairs for some reason.

Oliver was making no secret of his desire to sleep. Seemingly unable to comprehend why we'd kept him up all night, he was out cold the minute his head hit the mattress in his carrycot.

Which just left the pair of us, bleary eyed and snappy, sitting together and shivering over cups of tea. The miracle of parenthood in all its glory. Just a couple of days in, and Oliver already has us enslaved. Lindsay's adapted to servitude with her usual stiff upper lip – in fact she was well prepared for it, squirreling away an impressive collection of frozen shepherd's pies and other easy cook delights. Thank God for her, otherwise we'd be starving as well as miserable and tired.

Man about the house
The purpose of paternity leave

Paternity leave is a strange time. Until the new extended leave entitlement comes into force from April 2007, it remains a two-week window for men to learn fatherhood – like one of those intensive driving courses. It's also a period in which you are expected to cook, clean, entertain and support.

Neither scenario is ideal, but as it's currently the best thing on offer for most working men, you need to maximise the time – with a bit of advance planning you should be able to juggle between the two extremes.

Let's take the second one first – the return of the hired slave, a role that you might have thought you'd left behind in pregnancy. One cause of this problem may also be the solution – the hordes of visitors who show up unannounced expecting a glass of champagne and a finger buffet. Be mercenary – if people want to come and visit the new arrival tell them to bring their iron, or a casserole, or whatever they can supply that makes your life easier and gives you the chance to fulfil the first scenario of spending time with your partner and child. It's either that or get your mother-in-law to move in for a fortnight. I thought not.

Don't be despondent if your paternity leave isn't all you imagined, aside of your regular leave entitlements, you currently have the right to 13 weeks unpaid parental leave per child. This can be taken up until their 5th birthday. For more information on this, and on the new entitlements, visit the DTI website (**www.dti.gov.uk**).

As for me, well I'm struggling. I'm never very good after a broken night's sleep, and my mood is blackened by the knowledge that this will just be the first night of many. But at least we had a brief period of calm as he slept and we awaited the grandparents and the return of the dogs.

Animal instinct
Managing pets around babies

Some people take an extreme view on pets and babies – chilled by stories about suffocating cats and mauling dogs, they drag the pets straight off to the knackers' yard. This is a natural, overprotective tendency and is particularly common in fathers, though it's a bit harsh, given the effort the pet has put in as a surrogate child over the years.

But there's no denying that a child's arrival changes the dynamic of your relationship with four legged friends. Animals will accept a new pack member as long as certain niceties are observed – get visitors to fuss dogs before they coo over the baby, don't try to train cats to keep out of the cot, just make it inaccessible to them using a net, try not to change walking and feeding routines for them.

If pets don't feel the impact of the new arrival too acutely, they're less likely to react to it by being aggressive or disruptive. That being said, even if the baby is accepted by your dog, it may be more inclined to bark and growl at other dogs, passing motorists or falling leaves – it may think it's helping to protect the baby but this behaviour can escalate into all-out aggression against other animals and people if left unchecked.

Before long they arrived, the dogs rushing into the living room and sampling the strange new smells. One of the cats sidled up to them as if to whisper 'get out, run while you still can', but they were too focused on the deep breathing coming from the carrycot. We held them up for a quick look and a tentative sniff as Lindsay's parents hovered in the background, desperate for their chance (to look, not to sniff).

And they looked. In fact they looked with just enough noise to stir him gently from his sleep. So then they got to have a cuddle, too. This is a trick I've observed in my own mother with her other grandchildren – an ability to wake babies from 50 yards, but still leave them in beautiful moods so they cuddle snugly in her arms. There must be a granny aroma that's particularly pleasing to children.

I confess I was worried about this first visit. I had visions of lengthy lectures about how cold/warm/tired/awake/hungry he was, but just like Oliver himself, they behaved beautifully. Lindsay and I exchanged frowns when they tried to hold him and drink coffee at the same time and when they took too many photos, but otherwise it was a good first exposure to the outside world.

And, of course, they brought armfuls of presents which I spent many delightful minutes opening and playing with. The tiredness drained away – maybe fatherhood has its benefits after all.

"Step away from the baby, ma'am."
Controlling the relatives

Marshalling family and friends, whether in the hospital or at home, is one of your key roles in the first few days. They will behave like baby-crazed maniacs given the chance. It's your job to ensure that no visit lasts long enough to exhaust your partner and child, that no-one hogs the baby or spends hours taking endless flash photos.

You'll also need to make it clear that there's no visiting hierarchy – all access should be channelled through you, and you should make sure everyone who wants to see the new arrival gets to do so, and not just those who shout loudest or pester.

It'll be your task to provide food and drink for all these people and you can either adopt the bring-your-own policy outlined above or provide as little as possible – which is another good way to stop them coming back for more.

They didn't stay long as the midwife was due, but they got us to agree to another visit before the weekend. My parents are booked for mid-week, along with yet another midwife appointment. So much for time together as a family.

Our first meeting with the midwife since Oliver was born followed much the same pattern as the ante-natal visits. She spoke in knowing, patronising tones to Lindsay, explaining how tough it was going to be to manage everything alone, while ignoring me completely. She did speak to me once, but only to ask when I'd be getting back to the office. I calmly explained for the ninth time that I worked from home and so wouldn't be going to any offices in the near future. She gave a stifled cough, as if choking back vomit at the concept of a father in the home full time. And that was that for this visit – still, it reassured me that I hadn't become completely invisible.

"So, Mrs M, we meet again."–
Dealing with the midwife

In some ways, it was quite comforting to see the midwife again, like meeting a familiar old adversary. But in other, more practical ways, it was a pain in the arse to be reminded how insignificant I'm meant to be.

In pregnancy, her priority was Lindsay. After the birth, her priority shifted to the baby. I didn't really get a look-in at any stage. It was excusable during pregnancy, but not afterwards.

We'd always explained that we intended to share the childcare, but her attitude suggested we were making a mistake. Given that Lindsay was tired and preoccupied in the days after the birth, the midwife should have been addressing many of her comments and questions directly to me. That never happened, and it was a constant source of frustration.

From my survey of fathers I know that not all midwives are the same – in fact most are excellent – but a sizeable number seem stuck in a pattern of behaviour that's worked for them over many years. They need to change or be made to change if they're to be stopped from disillusioning another generation of fathers.

The midwife may have stayed resolutely the same but there are major changes afoot elsewhere in the household. After last night's debacle, we've decided to keep him in the carrycot where he's done most of his sleeping to date. It's wedged safely on to my desk at the end of our bed, so there's less of a distance to get to him when he cries. This means I can get up zombie-like and bring him to Lindsay in bed for a feed without ever waking up.

It also means that after months of careful deliberating and literally hours of painting, shifting, grunting and swearing, the nursery I created is redundant. I harbour a secret desire to move myself back in and reclaim my former study – especially as my current workspace is now dominated by a sleeping child.

We've temporarily abandoned the special baby sleeping bag we bought for him, preferring to stick with a blanket for now. We're pretty sure he'll be calmed by the sounds of our breathing and might even get a decent night's sleep.

The Wide Awake Club
How to cope without sleep

Sleep deprivation is a classic among torture techniques because it is so unerringly effective. You are likely to be severely tested over the coming weeks. When you're back at work, you might expect to be let off some night-time chores, but realistically you'll have to do at least some of the after hours care then or your partner will go crazy.

Your best bet is to get a good strategy for dealing with an 'all-nighter' in place now, after days rather than weeks. It took us a long time to find a rhythm, but eventually we divided our night into three four hour sessions of 'baby watch'. One of us would take the first session (9pm-1am), the other would take the second (1-5am) and then the first person would return to duty for the final session (5-9am). We'd alternate each night.

The middle session is undoubtedly the hardest as it's the most unnatural time to be awake. But whoever tackles that session gets a decent eight hours sleep – the other person is only guaranteed four hours minimum, but you'll be surprised how well you can function with so little sleep – just look at Margaret Thatcher (five hours a night). On second thoughts, don't.

* * *

Another disaster. Well, not entirely – the first night of the new arrangement was ok and we all got some rest. On the second night Oliver got a decent amount of sleep, but I was awake virtually all night again. Part of it was down to the feeling of inevitability – I knew he was going to wake eventually, so I was on edge waiting for it to happen. With Lindsay still pretty exhausted and in need of some decent sleep, I felt it my duty to get up whenever possible.

By far the worst thing was the blanket. Was it too tight, too thin, too thick, was he going to worm his way beneath it and suffocate? Every time he settled into a calm sleep pattern I strained to hear his breathing. I even got up regularly to check, twice waking him.

In the absence of fear over miscarriage or stillbirth I have become fixated with cot death. My fears have a similar basis – that some-thing devastating could happen to someone I love and I may be unable to prevent it. I'm in that dangerous area between knowledge and ignorance where I understand the basic requirements for limiting cot death, but these still don't provide the absolute guarantees that would make me comfortable.

While I've read everything I can find on the subject over the last couple of days, I don't feel I can talk about it. It's not fair to burden Lindsay with my paranoia. Though I'm fairly sure she has the same fears, they may not be keeping her awake at night and I'd rather it stayed that way. The philosophical attitude would be that if nothing can be done, there's nothing to worry about. But a quick search of blockbuster movie history shows that philosophers never saved the Earth from asteroid attack, so I'm happier doing something in the belief that I can say I tried. I just wish that I could worry in my sleep.

Thinking the unthinkable
Guarding against cot death

Cot death, or Sudden Infant Death Syndrome (SIDS), is a frightening prospect, but it is important to put the risks into perspective. SIDS claims fewer than 0.5 of every thousand babies (up to 12 months) in the UK each year. Advances have been made in identifying the causes of cot death, and while it is still a mysterious killer, there is hope that the battle is slowly being won.

There are various ways to lessen the likelihood of cot death. I've already mentioned the importance of moderating temperature so that it's never too hot or too cold in the baby's room. Never use loose bedding like a duvet with a baby – better to use a tucked-in blanket or a baby sleeping bag. If you're using a blanket, ensure the baby's feet are at the foot of the cot, so they can't wriggle down further. Newborns should always be laid on their backs. Smoking is another major factor – never smoke in a room that the baby will sleep in. Other rules are a bit cloudier – never handle a baby when you're extremely tired, for example. Not always easy to manage that one. It translates as 'don't snuggle up under your warm duvet with the baby'.

A lot of this may be common sense, but it clashes with previously accepted practice – look through a baby care book from the 70s or 80s and you'll find contrary advice, so don't be tempted to listen to your parents on this one.

It can be hard to deal with something so horrific knowing that sometimes it just happens and you can do nothing about it, but it is something you should discuss with your partner – it's highly likely that she'll be having the same fears and by talking them through you're a step closer to coping with the issue in the unlikely and unfortunate event it becomes a reality. For extra support, the Foundation for the Study of Infant Deaths has an excellent website (sids.org.uk) with more detailed information.

• • •

Today gave us something else to worry about – the return of the midwife. Seeing her every couple of days is going to be tough, especially if today's performance is anything to go by.

On the plus side she remembered to bring the scales. She put Oliver on and studied the display with a frown. We were both watching her anxiously and something was definitely wrong. She took him off then put him back again.

"Something the matter?" I said, hesitantly. You could say that. According to the scales, Oliver has lost a pound and a half in the five days since birth. She explained that while many babies lose some weight after birth, few lose it at such a dramatic rate. In fact, she recalled, she'd only ever known one other baby lose weight at such a rate.

"And what happened to that baby?" we both asked.

"Oh it died," she said. "But try not to worry."

We sat in stunned silence as she sipped her coffee, safe in the knowledge that she'd managed to scare the living shit out of us. As Lindsay was about to speak there was a knock at the front door – my parents, bearing gifts. I stood, grabbed my coat and ushered them away from the door, down the path and back along the road. As we walked I tried to explain what was going on, but to be honest, I didn't have a clue myself.

On the one hand, the midwife seems to think that Oliver is a healthy and happy baby, albeit one who isn't taking well to breast feeding. But on the other hand she seems concerned that his weight has dropped dangerously. She even suggested that his generally quiet and calm manner is possibly down to 'lethargy'.

To me, walking light-headed in the autumn sunshine with my bemused parents, it felt like we'd been accused of failing to care for our baby – possibly with fatal implications.

I didn't know what to say to my mum and dad, they'd come to meet their grandson and were confronted with a scene of such emotional chaos they must have genuinely wondered how he'd made it this far. I couldn't even imagine what Lindsay was going through at home, still trapped with the Midwife of Doom.

Eventually the midwife drove past with a beep of the horn and a cheery wave. When we got home Lindsay was distraught. I wanted my parents to go, and if they hadn't just driven for four hours to get to us, I might have asked them to. It would have been a mistake, left to ourselves we'd have worked each other into a state of all encompassing misery. Instead we had to focus on the banality of tea and cakes, on smiling as the proud grandparents held our son for the first time, even though my instinct was to snatch him away and never let go.

They also injected a degree of logic into our fears over the midwife's visit. They felt certain that the mystery of the disappearing pound and a half lay in a misread weigh-in at the hospital. He was only weighed once during his stay, so it was possible his birth weight was incorrectly recorded. We like this theory, even though neither of us really believes it. It's certainly better than the unimaginable alternatives.

Aside of the fact that today has left us both feeling emotionally drained to match our physical exhaustion, the biggest impact has been on feeding. What began as a minor tussle has become a full scale war, and we're determined there'll be no casualties on either side.

I can see why so many women give up breastfeeding. The genuine belief that it is the best form of feeding for a baby is well documented. But no-one documents the frustration felt by both parents when their child struggles to master the essential skills necessary for its survival.

Lindsay wants to persevere which, according to the midwife, means no bottles as the rubber teats get the baby confused. The baby isn't the only one. I'm pretty mixed up as to how we are expected to halt his declining body weight but not resort to bottle feeding. It's like a sick joke.

I'm powerless – unable to feed him myself, unwilling to withdraw my support for Lindsay's decision to breastfeed him. All I do is stand around looking and feeling like a spare part once more. I thought that feeling would disappear after pregnancy, that once Oliver was born there was nothing that I couldn't do as well as Lindsay. I was wrong.

•   •   •

Today Oliver is one week old. If every subsequent week of his life is like this first one, I'll be either mad or dead within a year. If pregnancy felt like a rollercoaster, the week since birth has been like one of those fairground rides where you're spun around and around until you pass out and are then dropped a hundred metres into a pool of alligators. What? – There's no such ride? They should invent one, and call it The Baby.

Actually, the baby isn't the problem here. He's the only one of us who's still functioning normally. He's drinking expressed milk from a cup – the only way we can get him fed and not stuck on the bottle. The one significant advantage of this is I can now help out with the feeds, which stops me fretting on the sidelines.

The right start
Helping her through breastfeeding

While most fathers I surveyed were happy with the level of involvement they had with their baby in the first few weeks, a sizeable minority would have liked to do more.

The one area that's obviously a closed book to new fathers is breastfeeding. That doesn't matter if all is well and the baby's feeding happily, but if things aren't going well it can be extremely frustrating to be on the sidelines and unable to help. You have another balancing act on your hands – while you want to keep your baby healthy, now is not the time to be the 'master of your house' and insist the baby goes on to formula milk.

Breastfeeding is, I'm assured, a sometimes tough and sometimes painful process, but it's the best method of feeding by far. Your partner has this fact rammed down her throat at every opportunity by the hospital, midwives and heath visitors and the pressure can be intense. So if it's not working out and she makes the tough decision to give up breastfeeding, she deserves whole-hearted support, not a guilt-trip.

In this event, expressing milk into bottles is a viable stepping stone between breast and formula – the baby still gets all the nutrients and you get to help out with the feeding (and bonding) process.

All the worry over his weight loss was the final straw for sleep. We've both given up, and lie awake wanting to talk but not being able to for fear of waking him or raising new worries. We've almost exhausted our supplies of frozen ready meals and I'm in no mood to cook or make trips to the supermarket.

On the rare occasions that we have actually got dressed our clothes have become encrusted with burped up milk and they sit in a menacing pile in the corner of the bedroom waiting for one of us to crack and actually attempt the washing.

And, as there's a 'y' in the day, there must also be a visit from family. This time it's the return visit of the parents-in-law accompanied by Lindsay's sister. She doesn't have a lot of experience handling babies and she was a bit nervous holding him at first. Lindsay and I didn't want to intervene, but her parents got stuck in with criticism, instructions and advice.

It's hard to acknowledge, but I guess they also have to do some readjusting in their new role. In truth, I don't like to think of anyone beyond Lindsay and I having a stake in Oliver's existence, but that's a selfish attitude, governed by a desire to protect him.

I know that I've got to get better at sharing him. But not just yet. We went for a walk to give Lindsay a couple of hours rest – I pushed the pram and gave the dogs to the grandparents.

Even then, right at the start of our walk, I could see the steely gleam in my mother-in-law's eye. She wanted that pram, and she would do all that she could to get it. The dogs were allowed to weave around my legs as a trip hazard. The minute we reached any slight incline a third hand would appear alongside mine 'to help out on the hill'. Once she'd got the feel of that compressed foam under her fingers she was insatiable – it must have taken great will power not to shoulder barge me from the pavement and take her place as the rightful pusher.

I knew my time was short, so as we turned for home, I decided to showboat for a while, removing one hand from the pram.

I believe the right to push a pram one handed is a father's most important privilege. It's often mistaken as a sign of embarrassment or discomfort, but in truth it's the complete opposite – it's more like driving one handed, technically suspect, but accomplished with the air of total confidence that suggests man and machine in complete harmony. I've practised it during the short forays we've made to walk the dogs on the patch of grass near our house, and have now developed it to the level of art form. I've even begun to make 'brrm-brrm' noises as I push.

On this occasion, however, the one handed push was a fatal error of judgement. It allowed mother-in-law the space to make a two handed lunge for the pram. I then had to make it very clear I was going to let her push anyway, and was sure to criticise her driving all the way home. Oliver slept throughout – or at least he kept his eyes firmly shut.

He sleeps a lot in the pram; I guess the gentle rhythm of being wheeled through ditches relaxes him. It can be pretty annoying, given that we only take him out for dog walks on the off-chance that the neighbours will see us and rush over to say how clever we are to have produced a beautiful child. What might previously have been a five minute dash has become a half hour stroll, soaking up the congratulations of the neighbourhood and dragging our feet in the vain hope that more people will come out to see us.

Despite my protests before, during and after the visit, it's been good to have family over again. Lindsay enjoyed the break, I enjoyed the fights and they all agreed wholeheartedly with our inexpert diagnosis that the hospital/midwife/scales must be wrong as Oliver is a healthy, happy and very bright baby.

Tomorrow we'll discover whether he's gaining weight as the midwife returns with the dreaded scales. She's the last person I want to see, but I'm very keen to eradicate her miserable outlook.

Swings and roundabouts
Handling the post-birth blues

Putting aside the fact that you'll both be extremely tired and working pretty much on autopilot, you might also notice a significant dip in your partner's mood in the days following the birth. This can sometimes be misread as post-natal depression (see Information Panel in chapter three). In fact it's nowhere near as serious, and rarely lasts longer than a couple of days.

It's most likely to be down to a hormone surge which effectively overwhelms your partner with tiredness and emotion – leaving her weepy or exhausted. Watch out for it, because it's your job to give her the confidence to get through this particular trough, ensuring it doesn't trigger more serious and long term problems.

One great way to beat the blues is to get some personal space. Many new parents fall into a trap of doubling up on childcare, particularly when they're tired. There were many times when one of us could have been doing something else – reading a book, getting some sleep, doing the shopping – but we instinctively sat together waiting for Oliver's next instruction. With hindsight this was a terrible waste of precious personal time. Though it's early days, you should try to enforce a routine at home which allows each of you some space from the baby – even if it's just for a couple of hours at a time.

Tonight we celebrate his first seven days. I guess if no other positive has emerged from the worry over his weight, it has started to bond us as a family. We've been so low this week there were times when I confess I've suspected or even blamed Lindsay for Oliver's problems. I've no idea why as it's not based on any rational thought – I guess I've just wanted to lash out, apportion blame and appease my guilt. It's not something I'm proud of.

Despite all the fears we've tried to stay positive and focused – though it would be pretty easy to get despondent over the lack of sleep, the seemingly endless list of chores and the fact that life is one big routine, without spontaneity or deviation – a mechanical process of feeding, cleaning, cuddling, burping and washing. And there's the baby to think of too.

Chapter Three
Baby meets world

I'm a big fan of the midwife. No, not that one, but the wonderful woman who came out to see us for the first time today and told us that Oliver's gained a few ounces and is a perfectly healthy baby. She couldn't understand what all the fuss has been about. We can breathe again.

I feel happy we've been proved right, that there was probably some mistake along the way and he's doing fine. But I also feel angry that our first week as a family was clouded by so much unnecessary fear. Given that I can't do a thing about it, this is probably one area where the philosopher does save the day – time to move on.

We planned an adventure to celebrate our good news. We decided to embark on the first official Giles family outing – a 15 mile round trip in the car with a stop for lunch in the middle. It's a manageable distance, not so far that we can't rush home in an emergency, not so close that we'll be recognised if Oliver screams blue murder.

With the destination agreed, we began the simple process known as 'getting ready'. It works something like this: We feed him, change him and dress him. Then we realise we should take a change of clothes, nappies and wipes. Make it a couple of nappies to be on the safe side. But then there ought to be a couple of changes of clothes, just in case. I dismantle the pram and place it in the car boot. What about toys? Which toys will he need? We hunt around for toys that complement a 15 mile round trip with lunch in the middle. We find his outdoor outfit and his in-car outfit. We spend five minutes discussing the pros and cons of the pram and decide against. I unload and reassemble it.

By now he needs another change and is closing fast on another feed. Oliver is removed from his going out clothes, fed and changed. He is dressed again. I go out to warm up the car, Lindsay follows with Oliver and I return to bring up the rear with a shed load of baby products. With everything finally crammed into the car we're ready for the off. It's just after 3pm.

It will get better – we will get better. We have to, unless we want to eat off the afternoon tea menu for the rest of our lives. Having a baby in tow requires an incredible amount of forethought, and given that I'm prone to locking us out of the house and/or forgetting my wallet on a regular basis, I have a long way to go to get organised.

Oliver didn't like the car very much. I think he'd been too overwhelmed by his 'prison break' from the hospital to notice the first journey, but he took against this one from the start. We sang to him and whispered calmly, I tried desperately to remember the nursery rhymes of my childhood – without the rude lyrics of my adolescence.

It wasn't much fun, but soon we arrived at our 'lunch' destination, walked into the town centre, had a coffee and a cake and Oliver started to warm to the idea of being out in public. He was soaking up the sights, sounds and smells of a new atmosphere.

Walking back to the car we were stopped by a couple of old ladies wanting to take a look at Oliver.

"Oh," they sighed. "How old?" they chorused, sounding like a couple of Albert Steptoe impersonators.

Lindsay smiled the benevolent smile she reserves for the old people who flock around her like, well, like old people. "Just a week," she said.

One of them nearly fainted, the other took a step back into the road and narrowly avoided being flattened by a Norbert Dentressangle lorry. When they'd collected themselves, one turned to the other and said: "They do, though, these days." They wandered on, shaking their heads profoundly.

I assume they meant it was too soon for Oliver to be out of hospital, or for Lindsay to be back on her feet. They come from a generation where mother and child would stay in quarantined confinement until the infant was old enough to ascend his first chimney.

With my usual air of self-involvement, I take great offence at any assumption that my wife and child are in any danger being out in public just a week after the birth. Anyway it took so much effort to get them there, I'm not going to suddenly retreat back indoors on the orders of a pair of old crones.

•   •   •

In fact, over the last week we've gone to the opposite extreme, finding any old excuse to venture out – partly to get Oliver more familiar with the car and partly to escape from the piles of washing, rubbish and other sinister crap that currently fill our house.

The game of the name
Registering the birth

One of our earliest trips out was to the register office where we officially declared Oliver's existence and his name.

You must register the birth within 42 days, and if you want both your names to appear on the register you must both attend the registration or the absent partner must submit their details on a form available from the General Register Office. You don't need any other paperwork.

It's a touching, heart-warming tradition that carries a degree of sobriety, and though it's not your last chance to go back on the decision to name your child after the Premiership title winning squad, it does formalise your baby's existence.

There are benefits to this process (not just the free certificate and the inevitable intrusive merchandising leaflets) as it's also the first step to claiming child support, which all parents are entitled to regardless of income – you have to apply for this, and you'll need to send a form and the birth certificate to the Inland Revenue to qualify. This should also trigger payment of the Child Trust Fund voucher. Other benefits are means tested – for the latest information check out the Inland Revenue website (**www.hmrc.gov.uk**).

In another major step towards normality, we went to the supermarket today. Things started badly as the now obligatory crones swooped on us in the car park, craning their turkey necks to see him in his car seat. One of them was smoking and I gave her a filthy look. She continued to gawp and puff regardless, so I edged him slowly away under the laughable pretext of being in a hurry.

There must have been some special offer on baby products at the store today, because it was packed to the rafters with tiny, screaming bundles and their ill-tempered parents. The ratio of mothers to fathers was unexpectedly low, about four to one I reckon. That either means a lot of blokes willingly take time out of their busy schedules to go shopping, or more likely they are forced to tag along if they want to have something to eat for the following week.

None of the lone parents with children were actually taking things from the shelves. Instead they were locked in detailed negotiations over which toys/sweets/biscuits/crisps would be sufficient to get everyone out of the place alive.

By studying the behaviour of other fathers I could see I was meant to be the fetcher-carrier, picking up products under instruction from Lindsay, while she pushed the trolley and kept Oliver happy. I wasn't doing my job very well because I was too busy being mesmerised by other people's babies.

I may be a touch biased, but other people's babies are hideous. Some of them border on the freakish – big jowly beasts that look like they've been drawn by a cartoonist with the shakes, tiny purple babies that are like those California Prunes from the 1980s adverts, strangely proportioned babies that bring to mind Mr Potato Head's features stuck on a Jersey Royal.

Some of them were so frightening I wanted to throw a fire blanket over them. I'm particularly troubled by completely bald babies – it feels as if their flawless pates are going to suddenly spin around 360 degrees.

While I've got over any fears I may have had about handling Oliver, I know that I'm still a long way from liking babies in general. I dread the moment when somebody asks me to hold theirs, or even worse, compliment them on producing something that looks likes it's been fashioned out of modelling clay and then left too near a radiator.

"You must be very...scared?"–
Competitive Dad Syndrome (CDS) Stage Two –
other people's babies

When you become a new dad there is a general assumption that you will now automatically like all babies. This didn't work for me, or for friends who still find themselves yawning whenever they meet baby bores at parties.

Instead, I'd say that I found other people's babies compelling – not just in their frequently odd features, but in mannerisms, even their cries and laughter were different from Oliver's and that was strange and interesting. I found myself comparing his features to these other children's. This involved a lot of unsubtle gawping on my part and furious jabs in the ribs from Lindsay.

Of course we all favour our own child, there's a familiarity in the features and manner that is both attractive and comforting. Making endless comparisons might be a bit obsessive, but it is part of the natural process of measuring your child against others.

It's a pretty negative trait, but everyone does it – and it does tend to escalate (see CDS Stage Three). What's important is that you don't start to take your own hopelessly biased propaganda too seriously. Yes your child is wonderful, no that fact doesn't need to be broadcast from the rooftops.

* * *

Since Oliver's successful weigh-in, we've been getting fairly blasé about midwife visits. They won't give us a specific time slot for their appearances, so we do our best to be around, but keep missing them. We return from a walk to discover short, terse notes enquiring whether everything's ok, and asking us to reschedule. I guess the little bit of resentment that still lingers over the weight debacle has made us question the purpose of these frequent visits.

Hopefully, the next appointment will be the last. A midwife is coming to sign us off and pass the baton of care to a health visitor. This slightly less starched version of the midwife will continue to check weight, offer advice on care and well-being and generally make sure all is well over the coming few weeks.

I'm particularly keen to ensure the handover goes smoothly. If the midwife thinks we need more time under her care, we won't get signed off. This has built the stress surrounding the appointment to the level of an examination or job interview. It's the first real chance for an outside observer to judge us as parents.

If all goes well, I can launch a charm offensive on the health visitor and form a better relationship than the one I currently endure with the midwives. If it goes badly, we're stuck with the midwives and the feeling that we're failing as parents.

•　•　•

It turns out there's no 'we' in sign-off. This part of the process was focused specifically on Lindsay's physical well-being. It was fitting that I was totally redundant in this final session of midwife care. Yet again she reiterated bossily that Lindsay shouldn't be lifting heavy objects and driving. Yet again Lindsay pointed to me and said that I was doing those things. Yet again the midwife struggled to bring her eyes to meet mine.

We inhabit different worlds – after months I understand that, I just don't appreciate it.

The health visitor showed up the next day, just to introduce herself and check out the quality of our chocolate biscuits. I made a special effort, even combing my hair for the occasion, and it seemed to do the trick. She was much more relaxed than the midwives, she wasn't in uniform for a start and didn't have that brusque, bustling manner that all midwives cultivate. I'd go so far as to say she was chilled out.

She listened to our ramblings with the patience of a deaf priest and then told us how delighted she was that we were planning to share childcare. This was attentiveness on an unprecedented scale. I warmed to her immediately.

Same shit, different badge?–
Getting to know the health visitor

Health visitors, like midwives, vary enormously from person to person. Some are traditionalists who'll speak to your partner in the third person as 'mum' all the time – e.g. 'And how's mum sleeping?' – and won't give you the time of day, some are very PC and will encourage you to perform Guatemalan paternity rites while embroidering a quilt. Most are somewhere in between.

They differ from midwives in the sense that they exist predominantly for the baby's benefit – they are the calm after sales service while the midwives are on the stressful factory floor. In my experience, health visitors are better prepared than midwives for dealing with parents rather than just mothers – ours was very supportive of plans to share childcare, and was very open and frank with us both. This immediately helped to make her more relevant and sympathetic to me as a father.

Even if you don't have the time, inclination or opportunity to see much of her, it's worth attending at least one appointment – this person will become fairly important in your partner's life over the next few weeks and months and it's worth introducing yourself to understand where she's coming from.

After boasting about our thoroughly modern parenting plans, I've actually started to give them some serious thought. These first couple of weeks have been totally absorbed by childcare. Every moment we're not spending with Oliver we are using to catch up on our sleep.

I've not read a book or looked at a newspaper – even my habitual scanning of Teletext for news on my football team has scaled back to a manageable couple of hours a day.

How the hell am I going to squeeze some work into this full routine? As a rule, I like to taunt my office going friends over their commute, dress code and the million distractions that keep them from doing any work in their workplace, but now I can see that leaving the house every day would have its advantages.

One mate of mine has only just gone back to work after taking some leave for his first child's birth. I spoke to him about the joys of getting a break from the nappies and the burp cloths.

"It's not as great as it sounds," he said. "You think you're getting back to normality, but two things hit you. First, you realise exactly how short of sleep you are. You've only got to fall asleep in a meeting or accidentally call your boss 'darling' for the cracks to show.

"Secondly – and this is the worst part – every single person in the office wants to know exactly what's going on at home. It's not just the women, all the fathers come out of the woodwork and start to reminisce. So you're forever discussing the things you're trying to get some space from. Then the advice starts, and the offers start to flood in – 'we've got a trike we don't need, do you want it?' You're in an impossible situation, if you try to get on with your work, you're seen as cold-hearted. If you give in to all the interest, you'll never get a thing done."

Maybe I am better off at home. I have to come up with a way of finding the energy and space to start working again. The most important thing is not to stress – Lindsay's maternity leave package is quite good, so we're not going to need extra cash until she goes back part time in the new year. That's at least three months away. And I deserve a holiday after all I've been through.

Duty calls
Managing the work/life balance

Unless you're the principal carer, a home worker or phenomenally rich, you'll probably have returned to work by now. Aside of the changes to the office dynamic mentioned above, this will also affect your relationships at home.

There's likely to be a marked increase in stress surrounding night-time – you need your sleep to function the next day, your partner needs hers to cope with the baby. You can both make convincing cases – just because yours involves earning money there's no need to come over all caveman about it, you need to reach a compromise.

There's other stresses – whether or not office life returns to normal for you, it is time out of the house and away from the routine of baby care. You need to ensure your partner has some time off planned, to break her routine with the baby – maybe the occasional afternoon off, or night out with friends – something that will reassure her that life isn't moving on without her.

Weekends are another potential flashpoint, as they were once your time to relax after a busy week, but will now be filled with the many jobs that are impossible to manage in the week. Your partner has the upper hand here – your work is just five days a week, hers is seven, so you've got to bend on the weekend time. At least it's good for bonding – you'll be surprised at how Grandstand can grab the attention of a three week old baby.

· · ·

Work isn't the only thing we've been putting off over the last few weeks. Our sex life was put on hold after about 34 weeks of pregnancy and it's stayed that way. Part of me (i.e. the genitals) really wants it to start again. But another part of me (the brain) worries that I'll get Lindsay pregnant again, that I'll hurt her, that I'll appear selfish, that we'll wake the baby or that she just won't fancy me any more. That's just one – albeit insistent – pro against a whole load of cons.

I don't know whether any of those cons would actually happen, but if I initiate sex, or even a conversation about sex, I'm making a big statement which my sleep starved, anxious wife might not be terribly keen to hear. It'll sort itself out, given time. For once the brain wins the battle.

"Not tonight dear, I've got a baby"–
Sex after birth

If, during pregnancy, you managed to keep your sex life strong, communicate all your fears and constantly reassure and satisfy your partner, move on to the next section. This is for all the men who found sex a bit of a challenge during pregnancy, and who are expecting an equally awkward time in the first few weeks and months of fatherhood.

There are two questions you should ask regarding sex after birth – when can we and when should we? First things first – you can resume sex as soon as your partner feels comfortable enough to do so, which might be some weeks. Don't interpret this as rejection – it's purely down to the trauma experienced by your partner's body in labour. When sex does resume, use a condom if you don't want to get her pregnant again, even if it's just days after giving birth.

On to the second question – if sex hasn't resumed on your partner's initiative after a few weeks, when should you broach the subject? This depends largely on how your partner is coping with the baby – that's going to be the first thing on her mind, and if it's a struggle she probably won't thank you for wanting to reintroduce the ultimate source of her stress.

But then sex isn't just about making babies, it's also a big part of a loving, supportive relationship, and that might be just what your partner needs while she's low. She may be glad to get out of being the mother and back into the role of partner for a while.

It's a question of judgement on your part, but it's better to discuss it in a non-pressurised environment than to stay quiet and turn it into an issue. Creating the right environment for sex can be tough – I'd recommend removing the baby from the room just for a while, or if the baby's bottle feeding at night, get some trusted grandparents to stay over and remove yourselves to a hotel.

Another reasonably compelling reason to believe that sex isn't the first thing on Lindsay's mind is the mild pain she's still getting from her damaged pelvis. We've had to go back to the hospital to meet with the physiotherapist. It's the first time Oliver's been back to the dreaded place, and if I wasn't acting as official chauffeur I wouldn't have brought him this time – given the high volume of sick people associated with it, I reckon it's the last place to take a newborn. I kept him clutched tight to my chest to ensure no killer bugs could sneak past my defences.

We weren't there for long, thank goodness, and the physio seemed happy with Lindsay's progress. Almost as important was the way she lavished praise on Oliver's immaculate behaviour. This is a great bonus of fatherhood – not only was he well behaved, he was well behaved in my care, which reflects back onto me. It's a win-win situation.

This explains why so many fathers live vicariously through their children – if I can turn him into a halfway decent left arm spinner or a predatory striker think how great I'll feel every time he mops up the Australian tail or hits a cup final hat-trick. He thrives, I thrive. Oh yes, I understand fatherhood.

In the waiting room there was a woman about to have a huge, disfiguring boil removed. No wait, it was a baby. In fact I can safely say it was the ugliest baby I've ever seen. I suspect she was bringing it back to ask for a refund. It was like an identikit of all the horrible features from the supermarket babies – purple face, wrinkled skin, domed head, angry whine. Lindsay jabbed me firmly in the ribs – I was mirroring its misshapen gargoyle expression and its mother was staring straight at me.

I had to keep the same look on my face and divert my gaze to something else, so she wouldn't suspect. I leafed through some crayon scarred Beano annuals with a look of apparent disgust. A minute later she was still staring. We left.

• • •

Slowly, ever so slowly, we've started to establish a routine. Certain members of the family have suggested that this is more by luck than judgement – Oliver certainly does seem to have settled naturally into a good pattern of behaviour. But I'd like to think there's an element of nurture in there as well.

Sorting out the feeding was a big factor. Lindsay expresses all Oliver's feeds and we try to stay one in front at all times. He's on to the bottle now – the cup feeding was messy and inefficient and I don't think Lindsay's nerves could stand feeding him directly from the breast. This way round, we know how much he's drinking and he still gets the right nutrients.

He feeds every four hours, almost like clockwork, so in the evenings he has milk at 9pm, goes to bed, we collapse on the sofa then follow him up to bed an hour or so later, he wakes at 1am, we get up and feed him, then it's the same again at 5am and 9am.

We're both getting at least our basic four hours' sleep a night. A few weeks ago, four hours' sleep would have left me as a grouchy zombie. Today, it's blissful.

Other parts of life fit in around this regime. We get up, get dressed, go for walks – I've even started to work again. The health visitor has continued the vagueness over appointment times, so we've ended up missing her on a few occasions – she's as adept at the curt notes as the midwife. We're mobile, we're assured and we've got a plan. In short, I guess we're getting confident.

• • •

Confidence gets your chin up, but only so that you won't see the banana skin on the pavement. This morning Lindsay had a lie-in. I fed the boy without drama, then he and I watched the cricket scorecards on text with rapt attention. All was calm. Then Oliver's face went red and a rumble came from his nappy region.

I sighed, collected the nappy changing stuff with the coolness of a pro and laid him down. The uncertainty of that first change was a distant memory.

I cleaned him up and was reaching for the fresh nappy when his sprinkler system went off and sprayed liberal amounts of wee around the room. I was reaching for the cotton wool when his bowels erupted, showering the remainder of the room and my legs. I was reaching for a towel when he burped, sending a delicate arc of milk from his mouth. Then suddenly there was more of the sticky greenish-brown slime. So much poo. "Lindsay," I screamed. "Help."

She sprinted down the stairs, and arrived ashen faced at a scene of chaos. Oliver was floating serenely in a congealing mixture of bodily fluids and I was shaking my head and mopping furiously. "It's coming out of everywhere," I sobbed. "It just won't stop."

Fortunately the relief that I hadn't broken her son counteracted the fury she must have felt at being scared half to death by my blood-curdling scream. She elbowed me out of the way and got things sorted. Oliver's not yet smiled at me, but I swear he's frowned a dozen times. I'm fairly sure I heard him tut once.

This nappy from hell is a warning that I shouldn't start getting overconfident. It's a valuable lesson and one that will carry me through the next week or so of health visitor and doctor checks before the fateful day that sees us released into the world as fully functioning, independent parents.

• • •

We've not seen our GP since Lindsay was about 20 weeks pregnant. So much seems to have changed in that time it was refreshing to speak to someone who had no opinion on the manner of Oliver's upbringing. All she cared about in this six week check was whether he was progressing as expected (he was) and whether Lindsay was getting back to good health (she was). It was a welcome, highlight free confirmation of progress.

After poking, prodding and weighing Oliver, she left him naked on the change mat. Before I could say 'you don't want to do that' he'd pissed all over a wide range of medical supplies. All in all, a satisfactory appointment.

The health visitor's sign-off was an altogether stranger experience. Lindsay was asked a series of simple questions on a sliding points scale, rather like those 'are you a great lover?' tests in glossy magazines. But the subject of this test was a bit more mundane, bleak even. 'Have you contemplated hurting your baby?' – score one point. 'Have you actually hurt your baby?' – score zero points.

At first glance, the idea of the sign-off test appears to be catching out all the suicidal, manically depressed mothers who have hitherto put on a brave face but who just can't resist surveys. It's more likely this is an acknowledgment by the health visitors that they don't have enough time to notice things going seriously wrong.

A new low
Coping with depression

Post-natal depression (PND) is a very broad complaint. It ranges from feelings like isolation and severe tiredness right up to full scale depression. The spectrum of treatments is equally broad – from hormone balancing drugs to counselling and support groups.

Symptoms can start to show soon after birth or much later – the most common include exhaustion, tearfulness, disorientation and lack of self-esteem. Recognise any of these in yourself? Male post-natal depression is now recognised as a serious issue – for the first time clinics are beginning to offer dedicated support for men.

Most male PND sufferers become affected because their partner is suffering, but that's not always the case. So if you or your partner find yourselves suffering from these symptoms, contact your doctor or speak to the health visitor and get some treatment. It's not a sign of your weakness or inability to cope – but failing to acknowledge the symptoms could lead to serious problems.

Fortunately Lindsay passed, or at least we think she did. The scoring system was a bit complicated, and given that the previous test I took claimed I wasn't a great lover, I've lost faith in the accuracy of such things. Most importantly it was enough to convince the health visitor that we weren't 'at risk'. With a clean bill of mental and physical health, we have graduated as parents after six weeks of thankless toil. Everything else should be a stroll in the park.

Chapter Four
Baby changes world

After six long weeks confined to barracks we are really going places – Oliver's first holiday is to be a UK tour of epic proportions. First stop is my parents' house in Sussex then home for a few days, then on up to Manchester to see Lindsay's sister.

This trip has been planned on an unprecedented scale – Lindsay has compiled lists of items to take – our dining table has been commandeered as a store for the various accessories and accoutrements that Oliver will require over the long weekend.

My role as defined in 'the list' is roadie and driver, which compares favourably to Lindsay's task of pacifying a baby and two dogs for four hours.

"Did we pack the baby?"–
Managing trips away

Welcome back to normality – or at least to something that resembles it. The first proper trip away feels like a milestone, whether it comes days, weeks or months after your baby's arrival in the world.

Unfortunately it can also be a millstone – your carefully crafted routine goes out of the window as you struggle to fit into other households. This struggle is partly logistical – on our first trip away baby stuff took up approximately 80 per cent of the available space, 15 per cent was dog stuff, leaving just 5 per cent for a shared toothbrush and a change of underwear (briefs). Almost all of the nappy stuff we packed for Oliver could have been bought at our destination and we overestimated wildly on clothes and toys, but we tried to plan for all eventualities.

The level of preparedness required for a short trip away is actually minimal – make sure you've got the means to feed, change and clothe the baby and that there's somewhere suitable for the baby to sleep at the other end. Everything else can be managed as and when.

The harder part of getting away is adapting to a different regime when yours is so clearly established around the baby. It can feel quite rude to be forever asking your hosts to turn down the heating, draw the curtains, turn off the TV or whisper in their own home – yet these may be essential parts of your home routine.

You can also feel pretty stressed about the noise emanating from your baby at three in the morning while everyone struggles to sleep. Get your hosts to bend on things that really matter to you – safety issues like temperature – and learn to adapt to those that won't change.

Travel is supposed to broaden the mind, and while our travels haven't always been a huge success, they have slowly introduced our son to a world outside of his immediate routine – and that can only be good for the future.

Packing the car was a bit of a challenge. Lesser men would have given up, but I didn't spend my college years playing 'Tetris' for nothing. It all went in, though I don't have a clue if it'll ever come out again, or if any of it will be recognisable when it does.

We had a few flashpoints over certain items, all of which I ended up conceding, but the one item that simply wouldn't squeeze in is probably the most important of all – the swing.

Ah, the swing. The greatest invention known to man. The friends who recommended it assured us that we'd come to adore it, but when Oliver rejected it on that first night I thought we'd wasted our money. How wrong I was. So many times in the last few weeks we've yearned with every sinew for Oliver to nap, and the swing has done the trick. It's magical and beautiful and I even forgive the ghastly plinky-plonky music it spews out. But it's huge and it must stay at home. I miss it already.

The journey wasn't bad, especially as Oliver slept through most of it. The worst part was my driving. I've become so negative and defensive behind the wheel, honking and gesturing like an Italian in a hurry. I'm aware of this automotive tic, but there doesn't seem to be anything I can do about it. My car, my road, my rules.

Somehow, in spite of this, we made it, unpacked the car before nightfall and relaxed into our first night away as a family. Oliver took a while to go off in the strange surroundings, but now he's settled, and we've a great dinner and a good laugh, our first proper meal in company since the birth. It feels good to be away.

•   •   •

What a night. Easily the worst since that first night at home. Oliver slept until about midnight, then woke wanting a feed and wouldn't settle again. He was really angry, very noisy and I was acutely aware that we'd have the whole house awake if he kept going. Lindsay was exhausted so she traipsed back off to bed and I tried to keep Oliver quiet. I went through my whole routine, rocking him and singing to him.

As the hours ticked by I changed him, fed him again and wandered around my parents' house, desperate to keep him calm. I thought about taking him out in the car, but it's never a foolproof answer. I needed the swing. I knew I needed it, and I suspect he did too. No amount of waggling him around could replicate the experience. When my mum came into the lounge at about 7am, I was dead on my feet. She took him and I crawled back off to bed where Lindsay and I both slept until midday.

My parents spent the morning walking Oliver around the garden in his pram, gently coaxing him to sleep. He got a couple of hours but not enough to improve his mood. Nocturnal life hasn't done much for us either – we're both a bit snappy, which makes us particularly unpleasant house guests.

My dad's keeping out of the way – I don't think babies are his thing. In fact he admitted last night that when I was born he took up doing the washing and ironing just to avoid getting roped into baby care.

He has a point. Much though I love my son, I'd be very happy to contract out the less appealing elements of his care – like nappies and midnight battles. It's hard to find nannies who just do the nightshift and are happy to be paid minimum wage, so the chances are we're just going to have to carry on sharing the burden between us.

While I moan about it, it's better than the alternative – I think my dad probably regrets not spending more time with his children as babies, but I'm sure he didn't feel there was much alternative at the time. Now that there is an alternative, I'm not going to shirk my responsibilities for the sake of a decent kip.

Chores of disapproval
Establishing a routine at home

Speaking of responsibilities and routines, the expanded horizon of a trip away gives you the perfect opportunity to reflect on the division of labour in the home.

It's reasonable to expect your partner to be focused predominantly on the baby up to this point, but if that leaves you with a large burden of washing, cooking and cleaning you're not likely to want to come home at the end of a working day.

If you can afford to employ someone to help with the chores, that's great – if you can bribe a family member to do it for free, that's even better. The important thing is that you spend as much of your time at home actually building a relationship with your child, not with your washing machine. Plan a rota of domestic duties and make sure everyone sticks to it – this might lack spontaneity, but at least it creates an air of industry and enshrines your valuable quality time with the baby.

Given that we're barely conscious, my mum probably could have offered to take Oliver off our hands for the rest of the day, but I'm glad she hasn't. Our families are forced to walk a fine line between being supportive and muscling in. My parents err on the side of caution, but I hope that's because they are confident we'll cope with the journey to successful parenthood ourselves. It would be an easier ride if they did it all for us, but it would take one hell of a lot longer to get there.

All this worthy philosophising is down to the fact that I can't understand why our son is so miserable. At home he's become a dream, a really easy baby. Everyone grinds their teeth with envy when we tell them about peaceful family trips to the pub or single feed nights where we all get eight hours sleep. But we come away and it all means nothing.

I can't work out whether he's upset because we've broken the routine, or whether he's picking up our anxiety at being away from home for the first time. I had no idea I'd find it this stressful – halfway through the first leg of our tour and I've completely lost the taste for travel.

● ● ●

I'd like to say it got better, but actually it didn't. I just got more practiced at coping without sleep and dealing with a frustrated and grouchy baby. While Oliver slept marginally better at Lindsay's sister's house, we had worse nights, lying awake and expecting the worst.

The main problem is the contrast between these visits and their pre-baby counterparts. Both destinations have been places we've gone to have a few drinks, enjoy good food and relax. Now we are left in no doubt as to the purpose of the visit – our hosts rush over to Oliver, pick him up and coo lovingly at him while we struggle in with the bags, cot and accessories. We've even had to make our own cups of tea. To be fair, we're not the same people any more either – I've become incredibly tense, worrying that Oliver will disturb lovingly prepared meals, or keep our hosts awake all night.

It's not his fault, he didn't ask to be dragged around the country visiting people, but if we can't find a way to manage it without sleep deprivation and stress then we'll have to stay at home for the foreseeable future. The experience has made me realise just how tenuous our home 'routine' actually is – we've created an artificial situation that makes him comfortable and makes our lives easier, but it bears no relation to real life. We've become prisoners of our own routine and if a couple of weekends away can trip us up so badly, I can't imagine how we're going to maintain this uneasy status quo.

On a brighter note, we're just a couple of weeks away from our first Christmas as a family, and we've decided to stay put. It's not a universally popular choice among the wider family, but given our dreadful travels, we don't see any alternative. Anyway, I want to be selfish this year, Oliver may not remember his first Christmas, but I will and I don't want other people diluting my/his big day.

•   •   •

This is a tale of two needles. Yesterday we went out and bought our

Christmas tree. It's ridiculously early to be buying it, but I'm so excited about Christmas I couldn't help myself.

We rigged Oliver up in his baby carrier and strapped him to Lindsay's front, facing the world. And he loved it. I know I'm frequently guilty of filling in an awful lot of blanks in his personality, but something about the trip clearly had him engrossed. Maybe the street decorations and lights helped, but it was the first time I've seen him acknowledge strangers – and he was definitely smiling. At one stage he even whistled 'Silent Night'.

Our tree is modest and guaranteed zero needle drop, which probably means it's already dead. Oliver stared at it with a mixture of wonderment and suspicion as it jogged along on the seat next to him on the drive home.

Hello cool world
Interaction with your baby

From around six weeks onwards, your baby's interaction with the world starts to increase – you might even get your first smile.

When Oliver started to interact, I was like a kid with a new bike on Christmas day, I wanted to get out and about and start playing with him. But while babies are more fun round about now, there are only a limited number of things they can do – and they can easily be overstimulated by the antics of an enthusiastic father.

This is especially true if you have a boy and want to encourage rough-and-tumble from an early age. Lindsay's dad was particularly keen to whirl Oliver around as much as possible, and while it probably wasn't doing any harm, it was agonizing to watch as an overprotective parent – and probably wasn't a barrel of laughs for the little chap either.

In the first couple of months, gentle explorative play is better for the baby –

musical games and toys with a range of textures to hold are great for stimulation.

If yesterday was his favourite trip out, today was most likely his worst – a short journey to the doctor for his first round of inoculations. In principle, baby jabs are an excellent idea. In practice they are an excellent way to give babies an early and important lesson in fearing the medical profession.

A jab in the dark?
Immunising your baby

Immunisation is a subject that's guaranteed to polarise opinion. Everyone sees the logic in it, but no-one can be absolutely certain it isn't harming babies in other ways.

The biggest bone of contention is MMR (Measles, Mumps and Rubella) the jab that your child is given around 12-15 months. Some research suggests a link to autism, but that contravenes government opinion.

It's a subject that you can research in detail, but in a nutshell your child is only safe if immunised. How you choose to have the drugs administered is a matter of patient choice – but opting out altogether is a terrible idea, dangerous for your baby, and for all other children.

Few parents raise objections to the first round of immunisations – given at two to four months. These are for hib, diphtheria, tetanus, meningitis C and whooping cough. It's normally a two stage process and may carry mild side effects like a slightly raised temperature and swelling around the needle mark.

The doctors' surgery was clearly having a mass jab fest, as the waiting room was packed with nervous mums and dads and edgy babies. None of us spoke, we all focused our attention on our offspring, making sure they were calm and relaxed. A voice would crackle over the PA, calling families into a side room. The assembled mass kept their focus and talked in measured whispers. Then a cry would ring out and suddenly the noise level would rise like an angry bee swarm to mask the screams.

The parents would emerge, clutching their sobbing child, heads down, and were sent on a detour of the waiting room to avoid upsetting the unsuspecting babies. Another name was called and the process started over.

When it came to our turn, Oliver gazed with innocent curiosity at the long suffering and much maligned nurse. She kept the needle out of his sight and it seemed to take him by surprise. For a minute it appeared he wouldn't even flinch. But then his face crumbled and his skin reddened and he bellowed. It was just the one cry, he was sniffling as we took him back to the car, but I felt like we'd been willing participants in his introduction to the cruel world.

The nurse warned us that there might be some side effects, but he slept when we got home and we figured he'd had no reaction at all. But then he woke up and screamed. He screamed until he was purple in the face and wouldn't be consoled or distracted or amused. He was a picture of misery and for the first time as a parent I convinced myself that he was seriously ill.

I wanted to drive him straight to hospital but Lindsay wanted to take a look in the baby books first. All they did was repeat the nurse's comments. By the time we'd finished faffing around and arguing over treatments he'd given up yelling and had gone back to sleep.

Lindsay went out to do some Christmas shopping and I sat and watched him fretfully, monitoring his breathing and holding my hands close to his face just in case heat was radiating from him. It's a miracle he didn't wake up again.

It's really shaken me up. He was only upset for about 20 minutes, but it was such a sustained and wholehearted display of misery that I was convinced something dreadful would happen. And I was hopeless in the face of that. Worse than hopeless – I wanted to take him straight to the hospital like all the overconcerned, paranoid parents I used to laugh at.

Why wasn't I calm and in control? Why did I have to make the situation 10 times worse with my own histrionics?

He woke as Lindsay returned, and while he's been a bit disorientated, there's been no repeat of the screaming fit. Next time I swear I'll know what to do.

● ● ●

Two months and a few days after Oliver was born we've had our first night out. Lindsay's dad was the babysitter and the occasion was pre-Christmas drinks and a meal with Lindsay's work colleagues.

We'd been to a few of these work socials pre-baby, and as a general rule I filled the role of little wife, chatting with the spouses while Lindsay and her colleagues enjoyed their break from work by talking about…work. Now Lindsay is a mother she has a link to the spouses, and I have the sympathy of the men. I'm not sure either of us is comfortable in these new roles.

Saturday night's alright (for sleeping)
Your shrinking social life

Back when I was childless and fancy-free, I used to taunt friends who were parents with tales of crazy exploits like trips to the cinema, restaurants and pubs. Their jaws would slacken as I told them I'd stopped out until after

11pm or stayed in bed until lunchtime. It was great fun, and I never tired of it.

The simple truth is one or both of you will lose a significant proportion of your social life for some time – and while some people aren't remotely bothered by this, others act like they've lost a limb. It doesn't matter which type you are, you need to get out and party again, if not within weeks of the birth, then within a couple of months.

It's important to your sanity and your stress levels, but more than anything else, it's important to your relationship with your partner. She may not be too happy about leaving the baby, she may even actively dislike the idea, but she needs to take it on trust that getting out is good for rediscovering why you're together in the first place. Don't be tempted to put it off, the longer you leave it, the harder it will be to trust someone else to look after your child.

Choose your babysitter carefully – adult friends or family members are good, if a little inclined to experiment with their own maverick baby care methods, teenage girls with Hell's Angel boyfriends are bad – somewhere between the two is a happy medium.

Lindsay had to work especially hard at the party as her firm has a new managing director who has never even met her. However much her colleagues might have built her up, his view will be coloured by the fact he's currently paying her not to work. Listening to the blokes around tonight, you'd assume she's on some fantastic stress free sabbatical.

I know Lindsay misses work and I know she's frustrated at not being up to speed with the changes in the company. It's contrived to make her feel like even more of an outsider. But she is, and so am I – despite my hearty laughter at the cynical jokes about women's work – because a major part of us is at home. We've changed, we've become more detached from the outside world, and perhaps less vulnerable to its criticisms and material pressures.

In the past I've watched this in other new parents and I've mistaken it for vanity or selfishness. At its worst it's self-absorption, at its best it's a kind of force field, a mutual strength of purpose.

We were the first to leave.

• • •

And so to Christmas. Lindsay and I have vastly different ideas of what constitutes a family Christmas. For her, it's a huge social gathering of the greater family, a chance to catch up with the uncles, aunts and cousins that you haven't seen for a year. For me it's immediate family only, lots of food, drink and presents – especially presents. We've had a good go at sampling each other's ideal Christmases over the years, but this year my model won hands down.

I haven't been this excited about Christmas for ages, and I can't really explain why I'm so upbeat about it now. I pestered Lindsay for days to let me open some presents early, but she patiently told me to wait.

Because there's a child in the house I have this sense that Christmas should be magical again. So all the old weepy movies have come out, carols are being played on the stereo for the first time in years, the hall is decked with boughs of holly and the door has a giant wreath. Oliver is unmoved, though he likes the carols – they act like lullabies.

On the big day everything went to plan – the food, drink and presents were plentiful. Oliver – exhausted from watching the present opening – slept quietly in his carrycot throughout lunch and woke just as I was sitting down with my port in front of the afternoon movie. It was blissful, if slightly unreal.

I'm already aware that it's the calm before the storm – and I don't just mean the forthcoming family visits. From January onwards, life takes on a much more serious edge.

•   •   •

First day of the new year and I'm in a foul mood. The parents-in-law came over yesterday and offered to look after Oliver while Lindsay and I went out to the cinema. When we got back, he was wrapped in about 16 layers of clothing and was crotchety and tired.

They love him very much, and I'm really happy for them to spend time with him, but they are obsessed with keeping him warm and awake. Since he missed his nap he was miserable and hard work all evening, and I wasn't doing a very good job of concealing my irritation that our careful instructions had been so wilfully ignored.

We got to midnight, toasted the New Year and went to bed – except Lindsay and I were up several times in the night with Oliver. So I spent this morning sulking until Lindsay's parents left and now I'm hiding at my desk, trying to find the motivation to start the new year in positive fashion.

I've got to do something about this petulance. I might feel as if I'm being a good father to Oliver, but I'm not being a good father to the outside world. I'm too quick to criticise people who try to help, and to condemn people who don't.

Part of my brain realises that Lindsay's parents are doing what comes naturally – they're attempting to care for their grandchild using methods that worked for them as new parents, which is perfectly reasonable. But that part of my brain is controlled by sleep levels – too little sleep and I begin to wonder how they could possibly dare to come into my house and not follow my instructions to the letter.

Like my hangover, the regret I feel at being so offhand with the family is taking a while to clear. They would have to do something monumentally stupid to actually harm Oliver, and that's not going to happen, so it's time I cut them a bit of slack.

This year's resolution is to chill out as a dad, stop getting wound up over things I can't control and learn to handle the family. That should keep me occupied for a while.

• • •

Finding things to occupy me shouldn't be a problem. What I need to find is time. Lindsay's been into the office and has hammered out a schedule for returning to work that involves going back part time from the beginning of February. She's starting off at just two days a week, moving to three in March and then to four from April onwards. That's more work days than we'd originally planned, but it's as much of a concession as she could squeeze out of her boss.

So in a matter of weeks life is going to change dramatically. I'm going to go from a supporting role to part time carer, then ultimately to full time with Oliver. I'll be writing in the gaps around my other duties, which is something I'm used to. But I haven't a clue how this is going to work.

Day care daddy?–
Your childcare choices

It's increasingly common for babies to go into nursery from around three to six months and stay there until pre-school. This gives both parents a shot at continuing to evolve careers and ensures neither feels left behind professionally.

This isn't what we chose to do – but I'm not going to stand in judgement of it, there's no right and wrong way to juggle the work/childcare balance, only the way that suits your situation. With both parents at work, there's a significant reduction in financial stress – if one person loses their job, it isn't the end of the world. But that doesn't mean it's the only option.

A significant number of men would like to stay at home with their children and this is a growing trend. It's not an easy option – it's more of a vocation than a vacation – but there is absolutely nothing stopping you from being an ideal principal carer, particularly if you approach this time with the energy, drive and commitment you'd give to any new job.

If you're both lucky enough to work in one of the few professions that encourages and supports flexible working, it is definitely worth considering this option. Under recent government legislation, your employer is obliged to consider your request for flexible working and either agree or provide you with a business case of why it isn't possible. With a bit of negotiation, you may be able to organise a day of work from home or a shorter working week. Check out the DTI website (**www.dti.gov.uk**) for more information.

Our ideal scenario was to each work a three day week, take on childcare duties for the other three, and have one family day together. We're still working on it, but when we get there it'll be rewarding for everyone.

Meanwhile, we've had more jabs to contend with. This time we bought some baby medicine as a preventive and gave it to Oliver after the shocked indignation of the needle prick had died down. It did the trick, no nasty reaction or afternoon tantrum.

But the damage was done after the first immunisation, when he developed a taste for the full-on yell if provoked. He uses it sparingly, but it can cut through metre thick walls. It certainly derails my train of thought while I'm trying to work in my makeshift study in the bedroom.

I've developed my plan to make a triumphant return to the room formerly known as 'study' – currently Oliver's nursery – and expand my empire once more. It's not just that my workspace feels temporary, my whole working life feels temporary. With the prospect of spending the majority of the week as Oliver's sole carer, I'm seriously wondering if I'll be able to sustain any work beyond fatherhood. Retaking the study would at least constitute a statement of intent, even if it wasn't then followed up with any actual work.

I put the suggestion to Lindsay, and she seemed ok with it on the condition that she got a decent wardrobe in the bedroom in place of my desk and that I had to do all the heavy lifting. It's a deal worth making – I'm going back in. I'll have to share the room with a bed full of soft toys and a suspicious pile of crocheted jackets, but these are small matters in my struggle to retain at least some small vestige of self.

Some people might think I'm overplaying my push for independence – especially as I'm yet to spend a full day alone with Oliver. But the rules of engagement are drawn, and he knows where I stand. Let battle commence.

Chapter Five
World changes baby

Last night I had a terrible dream. Alien invaders had identified humanity's essential weakness – an inability to resist the charm of cute babies. They'd parachuted millions of sweet, angelic little bundles to Earth where they were immediately adopted by happy, loving parents. But they turned out to be devastating time bombs and by the time we found out, it was too late.

No need to wake Sigmund Freud from the dead to discover the meaning behind that one. I'm scared of being responsible for Oliver – scared of what might go wrong if we're left alone together for any length of time.

I'm going to try and counter this irrational fear by facing it head on. Lindsay's going to be spending odd days at work before going back in earnest, so I have plenty of opportunity for short periods alone with Oliver before I have to look after him regularly.

At the end of this month I will come head to head with another of my recurring nightmares – dealing with the family – as we're planning an extraordinary 300 mile round trip to visit Lindsay's parents, my parents and then head off on holiday in Wales, where we'll be joined by Lindsay's parents (again), sister and brother-in-law. We don't believe in half measures.

• • •

This is a curious period of readjustment. Since I moved back into the study I've been intensely possessive over my working time, and really insufferable when I'm disturbed by noise from downstairs. That's pretty hard on Lindsay, who can only do so much to keep the boy quiet.

She's begun the slow and difficult process of detaching herself from him. We're working out ways to gradually wean him off breast milk – Lindsay's never going to be able to work in her ultra-male office environment and still express milk every day.

She's actually only had one day back in the office this month – and that wasn't even a full day. It gave me long enough to venture out in the car with Oliver for the first time.

After about five minutes I realised I hadn't bought a bag with nappies or any of the million accessories that are crammed into Lindsay's pockets, bag and shoes before any normal journey gets underway. But this was no normal journey – this was a badly prepared journey. I crossed my fingers and put my foot down.

As Oliver has shown few signs of likes and dislikes, I had to take a few liberties with the choice of venue for this first trip. We could have sat in the park, but it was hardly the weather. We could have gone to the zoo, but he might have been frightened by the animals. Much better to take him to a quiet, calm, dry and warm bookshop, where I could coincidentally spend a happy hour browsing for books. His mother must have briefed him before we set out, because he took against the bookshop almost immediately, shattering the 'no talking above a whisper' rule with a series of ear-splitting shrieks. He appeared to be hell-bent on testing his alarm, so after just 10 minutes I made some rash and unsuitable purchases, then wondered blankly what to do with him for the remainder of the day.

We drove to a lake, where Oliver watched me as I watched the wading birds and ate an ice cream. This isn't a common event in January, but it wasted another five minutes. Then we took the long way home. Total journey time – approximately two and a half hours. Total journey cost – approximately £25. I have to get better at planning days out.

The young and the restless
Managing time alone with the baby

It should be so easy to take care of a baby. They are small, full of wonder at the world around them and they make few financial demands. And yet I still contrived to make the experience stressful and fraught with complications.

The first rule of spending time alone with your baby is to understand the baby's routine – naps, feeds, etc. – and stick to it, even if that scuppers your fantastic day long trip to a baby theme park. Don't be overambitious and don't forget to pack all the essentials you'll need for even the shortest trip – nappies, bags, wipes, change of clothes.

Some of my friends, with the noblest intentions, try to make their time with the baby extra special by going go-karting or abseiling or something equally inappropriate. This time is not a test of how cool or responsible you are as a dad – that'll come much later in your child's development and the baby won't be impressed by your efforts.

The best bet now is to spend as much time as possible interacting with your baby, whether that means taking them for a walk or just sitting on a rug in the garden, it's about engaging in a simple, stress free environment.

If you're together for a whole day, or even a weekend, it's important to have somewhere safe for the baby to play while you're momentarily out of the room. Stern baby manuals will tell you never to leave the baby unattended, but they don't tell you never to answer the door, telephone or call of nature.

A decent, secure playpen is a must – you can get ones that fold down to almost nothing.

Beyond that it's simply a case of making it up as you go along. Don't panic if there's some friction – you can't reason with a baby, so there's no point trying to argue the toss, but they're predictable and easily distracted, so if yours is grizzling then change the subject and keep changing it until you find something that works.

Finally, make sure you know where the medicines are stored and where your baby's healthcare record book is kept.

Life seems to be a process of redrawing roles and responsibilities, with Lindsay and me both keen to keep as much time back for ourselves as possible. While the last three months haven't been too hard – certainly not as hard as the three months running up to the birth – it hasn't been all champagne moments.

Apart from the odd night out, we've had very little time together as a couple and sex has naturally slipped down the agenda a bit – especially as Oliver continues to share our bedroom. Part of the reason behind our holiday in Wales is to let the family look after Oliver while we spend quality time together before the new working arrangement takes effect.

•   •   •

It all started so promisingly. Oliver coped fantastically with a really long day in the car and only started complaining on the Severn Bridge. I was doing about 50mph and the wind and rain were lashing the car, but I could still draw from the deep reserve of optimism that accompanies the start of a holiday.

Though it took another two hours of driving through darkness and storms before we found the cottage, it was still worth it. The place was fantastic, Oliver went straight to sleep, we celebrated with a bottle of wine and went to bed full of excitement for the coming days.

It got even better in the morning, we used the indoor swimming pool and wandered the grounds. It was heaven. We were more relaxed than we've been for weeks, months even.

Lindsay's parents arrived – but still things were great. They loved the cottage, we all sat by the pool, Oliver even had a quick dip. By the time Lindsay's sister arrived things had started to get a bit tense. My resolution wasn't holding, and our very particular way of bringing up our son was clashing with the parents-in-law's equally deep held beliefs. They kept pushing him to do new things, to roll over, to play with the toys they'd brought for him – I'd rather just let him find his own way. Lindsay would rather avoid a fight.

We decided to get some space, and went into the nearby town for a wander. She urged me to be calm, just for a couple more days.

When we got back, everyone was in the sauna. No, my mistake, they were in the living room. It was as hot as a sauna. Oliver, woken from his torpor by our arrival, screamed his head off until I took him into a cooler room.

I looked like an idiot, huffing and puffing and generally expressing my displeasure in as many non-verbal ways as I could manage. The trouble is, I'm the one who looks like he's overreacting, I'm the naively protective parent who believes it's bad news that his son's been parboiled in someone else's care. Well, maybe I am overreacting. It's not a crime and the least I deserve is some understanding from those around me.

Like all new fathers I feel a sense of responsibility to my child, but I feel it even more acutely as I'm soon to be solely responsible for his welfare for large parts of the day. I have to prove to myself and others that I'm competent, but if I keep reacting so strongly to their attitudes and well meaning mistakes, I'm never going to manage it.

I'm stretching the desire to be a good father to the point of obsession, and there's no room in my philosophy for 'live and let live' – when I come up against similarly stubborn beliefs, all I can do is clash with them. That's not fair on Lindsay and it's not even fair on the family. Must try harder.

Quality time
Playing with your responsive child

Play and interaction with your child is reaching that critical phase where you're starting to have real influence. This can be good or bad depending on whether your influence is active (playing games, engaging whenever possible) or passive (just performing mechanical tasks at the start and end of the day).

No-one pretends the work/life juggle is an easy trick, but it's possible to make the most of a bad situation by maximising the time you do have together. From about four months onwards babies are real sponges for information, so activities like reading, singing and playing simple 'peek-a-boo' games have huge rewards.

If you can 'own' a particular part of your baby's routine – bath time or bed time are good starting points – then you can focus on making them as fun and interactive as possible. The more reaction you get, the more satisfying the experience becomes.

• • •

A couple of weeks into the new routine and I'm happy with life. Ok, so we haven't hit any bumps yet, but Oliver's napping every morning for at least a couple of hours, which gives me time to work every day. He wakes in time for a lunchtime feed and then the rest of the day is ours – and this is just two days a week. This full time care lark is a doddle.

Even the potential banana skin of weaning seems to have worked out ok. Lindsay started this on holiday, and I've been nervously following up. Oliver's not a huge fan of the concoctions I've presented for him to date, but then I find it hard to get excited about pulped fruit and vegetables. We were warned that the downside of weaning is smellier nappies, but so far they've just been more colourful. Pea was a sight to behold.

A solid start
How to help with weaning

Weaning is a subject that's still under debate. Some people think a baby should just be on a milk diet until six months – some argue that it's safe to start introducing some puréed food from around four months. In truth, it has less to do with time and more with your baby's inclinations - if the baby starts to show interest in what you're eating and doesn't seem full after a normal milk feed, then it's probably time to start introducing food.

The most important thing for fathers to know is that when your child starts weaning, mealtimes are no longer the mother's preserve. Feeding is great one-to-one time, and the novelty of being fed by dad will make the transition from milk to solids much more exciting for your baby.

Don't become so involved in the process that you develop a mania for stuffing the poor child with every morsel – from six months until two years your baby's still getting basic nutrition from breast or formula milk (as long as they are drinking around 550-600ml a day), the food part of the diet is mainly about experimenting with tastes and textures.

So turn the experience into really good bonding time, buy silly spoons and bowls, make silly noises, have fun and don't be tempted to eat it all yourself.

While the weather's still bad I'm not being too adventurous over trips out. I've allowed him another crack at the bookshop – 15 minutes this time – and we've wandered around our village as well as a couple of neighbouring towns. Nothing too stressful, nothing too stimulating. But I have big plans.

Oliver's developing a distinct personality as he gets more mobile. He rolls about on the rug in our lounge and he smiles and gurgles. Little things, but they all make the experience of being in his company more worthwhile. If he was just a static lump I'd get very bored with him very quickly. But we play and I read to him and everything seems to be going in, like he has a real thirst for information. God, listen to me, I sound like the proudest mother on the planet. No, the proudest grandmother.

"If you hold his picture sideways, it's a nuclear reactor."
Competitve Dad Syndrome Stage Three – the boastful dad

If there's one symptom that defines Competitive Dad Syndrome it's pushing your child's achievements. Everyone does it, whether it's via the Christmas round robin or a casually dropped remark about being in the 95th percentile for dribbling.

New dads together are like rutting stags when it comes to the subject of the first tooth and the progress of the crawl. We search for new and even more malicious ways to convince others that our progeny is a prodigy and that theirs is just podgy.

When Oliver was six months old, my dad made him a push along trolley which he wheeled around the living room while I supported him from behind. Lindsay took a picture which I later doctored, airbrushing out my hands so that he appeared to be walking unaided. This was shown to family and friends with a casual air, their expressions of amazement were brushed off with a dismissive wave of the hand. Do I feel cheap for pulling a stunt like that? Never. It's one of the greatest joys of parenthood and I challenge you to trump it.

Don't, however, make the mistake of taking any of it too seriously. All babies reach the same milestones, some are faster than others but this is ultimately meaningless – the only thing that counts is that they get there.

In my care he's developed some eclectic tastes. He's fixated with the high interest loan adverts on cable TV. It worries me that there's something in these ads that appeals to a four month old baby, worries me even more that he seems to think we need to consider debt consolidation. One of his favourites features Carol Vorderman of 'Countdown' fame – and that's another programme that captivates him. This suggests to me that he's developmentally advanced, while other children of his age are just starting to recognise letters and numbers, he's already living like a student.

The idiot box
Watching TV with your baby

There's quite a bit of snobbery surrounding TV – with some reports suggesting children should spend less than one hour a day in front of the box. You can't use the same argument with a baby as they aren't likely to be out kicking a ball instead and they do tend to stay in the same place for long periods regardless.

Television is good for certain senses, programmes with music can be very engaging and the variety of dialects is good for language skills. Visually, programmes that use strong contrasts seem to grab babies' attention – mainly advertisements and cartoons. I don't recommend it as a key teaching aid for your baby's developing mind, but it's a useful source of entertainment when you need a half hour break and you shouldn't feel guilty for using it that way.

Even though we're getting on fine and having fun, I'm still hugely relieved when Lindsay gets home at the end of the day. Looking after a baby of his age all day might not be too physically tiring, but it is involving. If he's awake there's no chance I can slink off to the loo to read the paper for half an hour. He needs me with him all the time, and that's a surprising commitment.

On the plus side, it's all great bonding time. Lindsay's started to notice distinct similarities in personality – we both struggle to get up in the morning and cannot cope until we've had our milk/cup of tea. We both err towards the theatrical when we've got a bump or scratch. We have a mutual appreciation of physical comedy. It's just possible I'm moulding the little chap into my image.

I don't think Lindsay's jealous of this connection between us. She enjoys working, it stretches her mind and it pays the mortgage. And I don't think it was working out with us all being at home over the winter – claustrophobia was starting to set in.

●　　●　　●

We had a fun family day out today, a trip to one of our favourite haunts – the hospital. We've been back a few times for Lindsay's physio check-ups, but this is the first time we've been for something relating to Oliver.

During one of her visits last year, the health visitor tried to conduct a hearing test on the boy. She explained that the test was very sensitive and would need complete silence – not an easy task when you live close to a main road and mainline railway. She did one ear, which was fine, then failed to get a reading for the other. She had to go to her next appointment and promised to finish next time. She was then ill and he didn't get tested for weeks. When he did, the test failed again and so began the conveyor belt of NHS efficiency – we received a letter telling us to go to the hospital for a more detailed test. And we started to worry.

So there we were. The woman conducting the tests was amazed that Oliver was so old – she was expecting him to be just a few weeks. She then asked Lindsay to sit and rock him to sleep so that she could stick probes to his head to conduct the test. This was never going to happen – the more she insisted that we just needed to keep him absolutely still and silent, the more he reacted.

The woman became annoyed – she seemed to suggest that we were deliberately trying to make the test fail and warned us that she'd have to make an official note of our lack of co-operation. Things were starting to get out of control – I immediately began to think of social services and court hearings. I got very annoyed.

Lindsay calmly explained the background to the test and then the penny dropped – this was a classic case of old-fashioned institutionalised buck passing. Something didn't happen when it should have done and we found ourselves 'escalated' and wasting hospital resources. The woman performed the simple hearing test that had failed in our noisy house and found his hearing was perfect. We went home and within just a few hours we were able to speak without gritting our teeth.

●　●　●

March has brought an extra day's work for Lindsay and renewed vigour on my part to find things to do with the boy. This has become more of an issue since he started to object to his convenient morning naps. It's a pain for two reasons – one, he still needs the nap, even if he doesn't know it and two, I'm no longer working on the days I'm alone with him.

Most days I make a start on something but he's awake after 20 minutes. Just to catch me out, he'll sometimes sleep for three hours, but that's only on the days when I've already given up and decided to play computer games instead. It's frustrating and I find myself getting annoyed with the situation, and tense for the rest of the day.

I've tried reversing the routine and getting him to sleep in the afternoon, but he's proving as stubborn as…well, as his father actually. The downside to creating a carbon copy of yourself is that you end up passing on the flaws too.

So in a change of tack, I'm abandoning work on my full time dad days, and I'm going to treat Oliver to an educational tour of the area. If that doesn't send the little blighter to sleep, nothing will.

• • •

Things got off to a bad start. Had I known the stone circle I was taking him to was only accessible through a couple of cow fields, I would never have attempted the journey. It also looked quite sunny when we left home, so the driving rain was an unwelcome surprise. That, the wind and the smell of cow dung combined with the overwhelming sense of disappointment one feels when looking at piles of broken rocks in a field. I wrenched my shoulder throwing Oliver's pushchair over a hedge one handed. And I paid a pound for the privilege.

After this cultural extravaganza, we went to see some former colleagues of mine on a local newspaper. They barely contained their astonishment at my ham-fisted social programme. But Oliver got loads of attention and cuddles from everyone. I suspect he enjoyed this part of the day more, though he was strangely quiet on the subject, pretending to sleep all the way home.

There was an interesting aside during our visit – one of the women asked if Oliver could have a Hobnob. "No," I replied. "He's only five months old." She nodded and thought about this, then said: "What about a Jaffa Cake, then?" This came from a woman with a couple of toddlers, and goes to show that people quickly forget about babies' developmental stages. That's why it's so dangerous to accept advice from anyone who claims to have been there and done it all. They invariably have a dangerous combination of self-assurance and poor recall which often adds up to wildly misjudged advice.

Undeterred by our disastrous start, I vowed to try again, this time with something a bit more substantial. So, after waiting a few days for the memory of the stones to fade, I took Oliver to his first castle.

Something bizarre happens to me between the planning stage and the actual trip that involves forgetting to pack all the essential items. So when we arrived at the castle, I realised I was nappyless again, and had brought nothing to drink or eat. The only accessory I'd brought was Oliver's enormous 4wd pushchair, still caked in mud from our stones tour.

On the drive, I'd been wincing in the bright spring sunshine. Getting out of the car, the first drops of rain began to drum on the bodywork. Oliver shuddered and braced himself. If the poor lad grows up with a pathological hatred of historical monuments, he'll know who to blame. We stumbled around the few areas of the castle that the pushchair could navigate, spent some money in the shop and headed home. The cultural tour is on hold.

Carry that weight
Travelling without the pushchair

Around this time your baby is going to be craving more variety from life than the view from the pushchair, but will also be getting pretty heavy. This was when we discovered the backpack – a tougher, more rugged version of the baby carrier that we'd been using since birth.

Oliver never really enjoyed the claustrophobia of the small carrier, and it was hot and uncomfortable to wear, but backpacks are better for you and the baby, if a bit cumbersome. When he started to rebel against the pushchair it was a useful option to have available – and it was certainly better for rough terrain and country walks.

If you're considering one yourself, there's a range available but I strongly recommend that you try them out in a store – some are easy to take on and off yourself with baby in situ, some require the help of at least two people to put on, making them incredibly impractical.

* * *

I feel like I'm being pulled in two directions. In a fortnight Lindsay's going to be working four day weeks. She won't want to be full time carer for the other three days – and if she was we'd see nothing of each other. So my working life is contracting to almost nothing. At the same time, Oliver is demanding more and more attention in our time together. Slowly and surely, I feel as if I'm disappearing.

This feeling's not helped by my treatment at the hands of the people I meet while I'm out and about with Oliver. The baby clinic, where I've been taking him for fortnightly weighing sessions, is the ultimate example of a place where I simply don't exist. We arrive in the waiting area where all the mums are congregated, laughing and joking together. I sit and attempt to make small talk. Everything I say is misinterpreted as a come-on or a put-down. I give up, fall silent and wait my turn.

It's the same story in the park or at the supermarket – it's obvious that I'm either there on the pull or that I'm some kind of freak who must be ostracised at all costs. I'm sure that with effort and application I could ingratiate myself into this community, but I guess that if I have to make all the changes then it's a club I don't want to belong to. I don't feel like a full time dad, and maybe that's part of the problem. I want the best of both worlds – lots of quality time with my son and complete freedom to get on with my work. At present I'm trying to juggle both, and enjoying neither.

•   •   •

We've been on our travels again, a repeat of the ill fated UK tour we did when Oliver was six weeks old. This time we hit Manchester first, for a visit with Lindsay's whole family to coincide with Mothers' Day. It wasn't anything like the previous visit, when we only got a bit of sleep. This time we managed none at all, and one of the dogs got the shits all over Lindsay's sister's new carpet. At 5am on Mother's Day, Lindsay was opening her presents, Oliver was finally getting some rest and I was mopping up crap. I have a suspicion there's more to life than this.

In case we hadn't learned our lesson, we headed for my parents' house for Easter. It was our last chance to get away before the onset of the four day week and we refuse to give up on trips away just because they unsettle Oliver's routine.

It was better than before, though he still slept badly and left us both morose and grumpy. Soon the invites will start to dry up, and then we won't have to worry about going away at all. We had just enough energy left in us to toast Oliver's half-birthday. So much has happened in six months it's almost impossible to remember what life was like before, or what we were like as people.

Chapter Six
Baby finds feet

April was a difficult month. I've virtually given up work, which has eased my frustration with Oliver. He's gone the other way – I can't seem to do anything to keep him entertained. I try not to take it personally, but I suspect I'm just not cut out for this full time caring business.

Lack of imagination seems to be my biggest problem. I still spend my mornings trying doggedly to get him to sleep – most of the time we sit and watch films. He's had a brilliant introduction to the history of cinema – he's slept through some all time classics.

For a couple of weeks the films worked their narcotic magic, then it all stopped and I had to find something else. A trip out in the car wasn't the answer as that's the trump card I always play after lunch, and a walk is my post-Countdown gambit. What else is there?

Friend or foe?
The ups and downs of fatherhood

Most things that you read and hear about fatherhood are focused on the tough yet positive journey to mutual understanding and appreciation. This suggests there's a gentle upward curve from immobile newborn to happy, responsive child. But that's not a fair reflection of child development, nor is it reflective of relationships in general.

There will be peaks when you're completely in tune and troughs when you don't understand each other at all. And that's fine – fatherhood is a marathon, not a sprint, and you've got to expect to hit the wall eventually.

Common flashpoints come when your child is teething or during a developmental stage like learning to crawl, stand or walk. Anything that alters your child's world view has a knock-on effect on routine and relationships.

So don't be surprised if a game you play or a method you use to get the baby to sleep suddenly stops working. It's all part of the evolution process and you either need to adapt to cope or just weather the storm. But don't take it personally – the key to fulfilling your potential as a dad is self-confidence and that means having the presence of mind to see which battles you can win and which aren't worth the fight.

Life is easier with something to aim for, and at the beginning of May we're going back to the Welsh holiday cottage for a break – just the three of us. I'm going to spend the week working and swimming and generally coming back to life.

Lindsay needs the break just as much. She's enjoyed getting back into work mode, but since starting four day weeks she's been put under a lot of pressure to go back full time. Her company keeps messing around with her salary – they say that her part time status has confused the system. I suspect there's some resentment that she's being allowed flexibility – the stupid thing is that if you asked the average bloke if he'd want to work less time for less money he'd probably say no. But because she appears to be getting something they aren't, they don't like it. Sheep.

The other thing she finds hard is getting home late at night and having Oliver dumped on her lap while I scurry off to get some work done for an hour or so. Most of the time she's with him he's either sleepy, dopey or grumpy. Life is out of balance right now and we're all suffering the consequences.

The thing I fear most of all is the effect my negative mood as main carer is having on Oliver. I still don't feel like I'm a part of any community of parents. We persist with the sullen visits to the baby clinic, but I'm not getting anywhere with the mums. I chat to the neighbours and Oliver loves seeing the children run around our street, but he's five years younger than the nearest one and still virtually immobile. I'd try taking him to mother and baby clubs, but I'm a bit scared of being ignored and really scared of how I will react if other children hurt or upset Oliver.

Did she fall or was she pushed?
Competitive Dad Syndrome Stage Four – interacting with other children

My biggest fear as a self-confessed sufferer of Competitive Dad Syndrome is my son's interaction with other children.

In common with many fathers I know, I've developed an American Foreign Policy approach to interaction – I want my child to mix with the world, but I also want them to acknowledge his special status. Unfortunately, with this approach, you just end up with a play park or toy shop filled with 'special' kids trying to dominate each other and a group of competing fathers egging them on.

The main problem with interaction is that it's too much like the cruel and cynical world of real life – and it's the first time your child shows their own personality to strangers. You want this to be a good experience, not one that involves a bop on the nose from a big kid or a telling-off from a concerned parent. But you're powerless to influence the outcome – it's like winding up a toy. All you can do is point it in the right direction, let it go, watch and hope – nature and gravity handle the rest.

Of course, there's also the issue of other children, specifically how to set about discouraging them from picking on your child without finding yourself picked on by a bigger daddy. Discretion and tactful intervention are the best bets – never try to punish a stranger's child. Simply talking to them is normally enough to make them clam up and run off to safety. Or maybe that's just me.

It's hard to tell whether Oliver's apparent frustration with life is a direct result of my dull efforts to amuse him, whether it's just a phase, or whether he's rejecting me out of hand. I should have watched my Hollywood blockbusters more closely – it seldom pays to meddle with the forces of nature. Maybe I'm not genetically pro-grammed to care for Oliver and he's not set up to rely on me for care. If that's true, we're bound to clash – and we do.

•　　•　　•

We've had a great trip away – our first successful family holiday. Though nothing much has changed as a result of all the talking we did on holiday, we've decided that a little effort now will be reward-ed later. At least we damn well hope it will.

For me to make more effort I need a bribe, and we have agreed to increase the entertainment budget a little, so Oliver and I are going to have some slightly more adventurous trips out. We've got zoo membership, National Trust membership and a year long pass to the safari park. We're going to sightsee until we drop.

This cavalcade of heritage and amusement isn't going to ease Lindsay's headache at work, but it'll mean she's less likely to come home to a desperate husband and a bored child.

•　　•　　•

Things have become a bit easier. I'm still prone to forgetting essen-tial items for our trips out, we're still followed around the country-side by a malignant rain cloud. Oliver is still faintly mystified by the places I take him. But life is at least varied.

It would be even better if we had some people to talk to. We wander up and down the patch of grass along our road hoping to catch the eye of some poor sod for me to engage in conversation for an hour or so. The front gardens of all our neighbours' houses have become overgrown wastelands as people shelter round the back to avoid me. Curtains twitch nervously as we approach. I'm both bored and boring.

As with so much of my life, this period of childcare would have been wonderful and successful had I thought about it first. But as it is, I'm stuck with what I've got and forced to make the best of it.

On the horizon is a significant glimmer of hope and bonding opportunity rolled into one. Father's Day is nearly here – and hard on its heels is the European Football Championships. Our first tournament.

• • •

In an act of clear encouragement, Oliver bought me a novelty football for Father's Day. It was a good day – though it still seems totally unreal to think of myself as a father. Talking to my dad about Oliver is such a weird development, and yet I can't get enough of the excitement I feel when talking about 'my son', or 'my boy'. It makes me sound so grown up.

Which, obviously, is why I took him straight to the sports shop to purchase matching England kits. On the day of the first game, we paraded around the living room in our Red and Whites, kicking the novelty football with great enthusiasm. And then Oliver went to bed, I watched the game, we lost and I swore bitterly.

He was awake for the next game, but was very tired. He screamed with terror every time we celebrated a goal or shouted at the ref. His face was crumpled in misery and was as red as his shirt.

Suddenly, I felt terribly guilty for forcing him to play along with something he neither enjoyed nor understood.

Sitting with my son on my knee cheering our team to glory is one of the great clichéd images of fatherhood I pictured before he was born – it's all about me and nothing to do with him, or with reality. It'll never happen, at least not in the way I imagine it, because life isn't about predictable, scripted experiences. If I want him to grow up blue, he'll grow up red and vice versa – and if I try to determine his behaviour I'll fail dismally. A bit like the football team, then.

•   •   •

Life has suddenly turned on its head. Lindsay has become increasingly frustrated with her work. I think they were expecting the pre-baby Lindsay to miraculously reappear and start taking charge all over again. But that's not happened and it's frustrated her, frustrated them and has made working part time almost impossible. With no alternative, she's decided to leave her job.

Before she became pregnant we built up some savings to cope in the event of her not returning after maternity leave. It's a great relief to have that buffer, especially as I'm now the principal wage earner. Last time I sent in a tax return the Inland Revenue sent back a food parcel. I don't make enough money to cover the cost of the electricity I'm using to write this sentence.

My wage was never meant to be the sole source of our income, but now it has to be. To keep us afloat I need to be dynamic, focused and driven. Time to sell the house.

Actually, there is another prospect on the horizon – though not a hugely profitable one. I've managed to get work at the university summer school where I taught last year. It's only part time at first, and lasts just a couple of months, but it fulfils the main objective of putting off any meaningful decisions over what to do next.

· · ·

Things are going ok. I got through the part time hours no problem – Lindsay and the boy love being together again and they've been off for long walks in the mornings while I've been at the college. In the afternoons we've been going out as a family. Yet again we found ourselves in the blissful, unreal environment we enjoyed for those first few months.

Then the full time days started and the dynamic shifted once more. During last year's tutoring, I was conscious not to mention Lindsay or the pregnancy. Many of my students were Japanese, and they can be very earnest about their study. Anything that suggests the tutor is not one hundred per cent focused can lead to problems. So I was professionalism personified.

This year, I tried. I waited until well after morning break on day one before getting out my photos of Oliver. I am unashamedly, boringly proud of him and I'm always happy to interrupt lessons to talk about his every waking moment. I'm away from him for a matter of hours each day and yet I miss him terribly. This is particularly costly on the days out that form part of the course, which I use as an excuse to load up with souvenirs for my little boy – so much for the principal wage earner.

After moaning endlessly for three months about looking after Oliver, I've suddenly become an expert in childcare. I offer advice to Lindsay at every opportunity. She replies with different, slightly more direct and certainly more painful offers.

Notwithstanding my wittering, she's been having a few problems looking after Oliver during these full days. He's reached the age where he wants to do everything, but is capable of almost nothing.

He crawls and babbles, but longs to walk and speak. He has boundless energy and a complete inability to take naps on demand.

He's also going through a teething marathon which started in May and has rolled on for a couple of months. On the downside he's often grumpy and his carefully structured sleep routine has slipped a bit, but on the plus side teething has given us a 'one size fits all' excuse for misbehaviour. Tantrum in the street? He's teething. Destroying his granny's latest gift? He's teething. Launching a pre-emptive nuclear strike on Moscow? He's teething. By the time we've finished using this excuse Oliver will be a teenager and will have something in the region of five thousand teeth.

● ● ●

Last weekend marked the mid-point of my full time teaching and Saturday was a gorgeous summer's day. Lindsay and I took Oliver down the road to one of the local pubs, where we sat in the sun and shared a bottle of wine. Oliver drank his juice. All was right with the world. Lindsay was relaxed and content, I was making some money. Oliver was well and happy. Why the hell didn't I suspect something?

Saturday night he went to bed with no problems. In the middle of the night he woke and was violently sick all over his cot. We took him downstairs and he was sick again a couple more times. It was horrible to watch, but eventually he calmed down enough to settle back to sleep. We lay awake and listened to him for hours.

Sunday he seemed a little better. He didn't eat or drink much, but he wasn't throwing up. Whatever was upsetting him seemed to have passed. On Monday he was worse. He was sick again and this time Lindsay decided to take him to the doctor. I was at work, but my mind was at home. The doctor said it was a bug and that he'd be ok. Relief all round.

By Tuesday he'd got much worse. He barely woke all day and when I got home from work, he sat on my lap, ate a rusk and promptly threw it back up all over my trousers. We headed for the doctor again and this time he wasn't so sure all was well. He told us to go straight to the hospital, and gave us a note to pass to the people in the children's ward. Oliver clung to us, pale, limp and spaced out. I felt sick too, and very, very empty.

Emergency ward Zen
Staying calm in hospital

No father wants to imagine the trauma and pain involved in a medical emergency for their child. But it's a fair bet that sometime in the next few months and years something will happen that leaves you facing your fears in a hospital.

Whether it's an overnight stay, or a quick (quick? ha!) trip to casualty, your role in this scenario is closely allied to the job you performed during your partner's labour. You need to be the rock, the source of comfort and stability, regardless of your internal fears.

Assuming your partner is focused on your baby's well-being, you'll have to keep a line of communication going with medical staff – and that means keeping your head. Even in the slightly more relaxed surroundings of a ward, the staff are under extreme pressure and they shouldn't be sidetracked or dominated without good reason. At the same time, you've got to look after your child's needs – and you aren't there to make lifelong friends. If you have to complain or gee people up, try to be firm and calm and never aggressive.

If your partner is anything like Lindsay, you'll also have to remind her to eat, drink and sleep. She'll need a break from her vigil, but might be reluctant to take one – be firm and tactful.

Beyond this supporting role there's little you can practically achieve once you're in the hospital. That can leave you feeling a bit redundant, or even guilty but, harking back to the delivery suite again, your active presence is all that's required.

At the hospital I almost broke my strict 'no murdering the nurses' rule. We stumbled onto the ward through the wrong entrance, Oliver was on his hands and knees, throwing up all over the floor when a nurse approached, firstly to tell us that we'd come through the wrong door and then to say that she thought Oliver looked unwell.

"Yes," I said, just about choking back the words 'no shit, Florence'. "Can you help us, then?" I added.

"Well I'm not actually on duty yet," she replied. She did, honestly. And I got up from where my son was coughing and spluttering on the floor and I wrenched her head clean off and kicked it down the corridor. Something in my eyes must have hinted at that outcome, because she was suddenly on duty and ready to take us seriously.

Oliver was almost lifeless. We laid him on the bed and he barely moved. His skin was ashen, his eyes were sunken and he was unresponsive. Even the newly available nurse was worried. After much prodding and poking by doctors it was decided he should be put on a drip. He was taken away to have a needle inserted in his arm. Lindsay went with him. I wouldn't have been able to stand it. Pathetic, I know, but this was not the time for false heroism.

I could hear his screams from across the ward. I didn't know he had it left in him. When they came back about 15 minutes later, his arms and legs were bandaged from all the wounds they'd made trying to find a decent vein.

The nurse brought in the drip and its monitor. This kept stalling and having to be reset. With a skeleton staff working overnight, we were waiting five minutes or more every time for the staff to come and deal with the machine, which emitted a piercing whine when it wasn't happy. And each delay meant it would take longer to hydrate him. My fraying nerves couldn't stand it. The doctor came back and checked on Oliver. He said it was simply a case of waiting to see what effect the drip would have. He offered us no comfort, but he didn't seem unduly worried either. He asked us what Oliver's last meal had been. When we said it was a rusk, he replied: "Oh lovely, I'm 32, but I still like rusks."

My jaw dropped. Thirty-two? That's my age, and I haven't a clue what to do to bring my son back to health. I'm desperate and anxious in equal measures and the responsibility for care of our child has been passed to a teenager, a trainee. I wanted to demand a doctor with at least 50 years' experience. I waited until he'd gone and I told Lindsay that we should complain. She told me I should go home. I went home.

This morning there wasn't much change. Lindsay barely slept last night, and nor did I. The world has a surreal, dreamlike hue. I've been feeling ill, but Lindsay's well of sympathy has been drained by the beeping of the faulty drip monitor and another lengthy, painful attempt to get Oliver's drip needle repositioned.

After sitting in silence for a couple of hours, I went home again. I was feeling much worse. I emptied my stomach's contents through every available orifice and sat in the bathroom shivering. I stared at my reflection in the mirror – my lips were blue. I took some tablets and laid on the sofa.

When I woke a couple of hours later I felt much better, so I went back to the hospital. Oliver was sitting on Lindsay's lap when I arrived; he looked up at me and smiled and my heart shattered.

By way of a parting shot, the doctor told us that Oliver has been suffering from some kind of bacterial bug, possibly even meningitis, but that he'll be fine with a few days' rest. My immediate instinct was to complain that we should have been told this before now. But then I remembered my erratic behaviour of last night and I was grateful to them for keeping a lid on my panic for another 24 hours.

Until these last few days, I wouldn't have believed there was anything that parenthood could throw at us which we couldn't handle. I thought we knew it all – that we'd built the confidence, the experience and the mutual knowledge to deal with every situation. How could I have been so wrong?

Oliver's illness might have knocked my confidence, but it's going to stop me taking him for granted. When my summer school ends I'll be a better father, more fun, more responsible, less fretful and stressed. I'll double the number of pictures in my wallet and triple the extent to which I bore strangers. I'll do whatever it takes, just as long as he stays safe and healthy.

• • •

The scare over Oliver's health has been a setback. It's a reminder of those first few weeks when we worried over every little thing, every speck of dust or dirt. Though he's crawling and clambering all over the house, we follow close behind, fearful that he will pick up some debilitating bug.

It's hardly fair to use my son's illness as an excuse for my laziness, but over the last month I've spent a lot of time with him. It's partly due to the guilt I feel at letting him get ill, and partly to Lindsay needing a well earned break from full time childcare.

Despite the occasional difficulty – 'He's teething' – Lindsay and Oliver have really bonded during these summer months together. Maybe my desire to be with him now is also a wish to stay up to speed with his development. I'm delighted things have changed, that Lindsay is at home, but I'm sad that my time with Oliver wasn't more of a success. I miss the closeness that we shared, even when things weren't going well.

He's got a couple of major milestones coming up, both on the same day. We're throwing him a lunchtime party for his first birthday and then, in the evening, we're taking him on the ferry to Ireland for his first trip overseas. It might be wonderful, it might be a disaster.

Spread your wings
Travelling abroad with the baby

Overseas travel with a baby can be a great experience, but only if you've made adequate provision.

You may struggle to find exact matches for baby food, formula milk and nappies in foreign shops, so if you're attached to a particular brand, take it with you. If you're going on a long haul flight or boat trip, try to get confirmation that a cot will be provided – you don't want to be carrying the baby for 10 hours. Some travel companies will book a cot for you, others prefer to watch parents fight it out in a first come, first served gladiatorial contest. If you don't fancy that, take your own travel cot.

You'll always need travel insurance – and make sure everyone's covered – but if you're just travelling in the EU, you can also apply for a European Health Insurance Card (which replaced the old E111 form in September 2005) which gives a significant discount in healthcare charges in member states. Details can be obtained from Post Offices and travel agents. Remember that you need to apply for each family member. Further information on travel – including vaccination of children and babies, can be obtained from the Foreign and Commonwealth office (**www.fco.gov.uk**).

•   •   •

Or it might be both. Unlike his quiet first day in the world, his first birthday has been a spectator sport. Both sets of grandparents secured ringside seats, lending the event a competitive edge.

The grandfathers were dignified and sedate, with just the odd rustle of newspaper telling us they were still awake. But the grannies rolled up their sleeves and went head-to-head in an old-fashioned bout of 'Oliver Monopoly'. It's a compelling, sometimes gruelling sport, and I'm surprised Sky hasn't snapped up the TV rights. It was good natured stuff and Oliver had a wonderful time basking in all the attention.

Then it was present time, and the grannies retreated to their base camps. I sat on the floor with Oliver as the grandparents took it in turns to produce larger and larger presents, each trumping the last, until he and I were lost in a sea of wrapping and plastic activity sets.

Finally it was time for lunch – a sumptuous spread produced by Lindsay. All this attention grabbing had given Oliver an appetite and he ploughed into his sandwiches and cake. After five minutes of happy munching we were all congratulating ourselves on a decent party. And to cap it all Oliver fell asleep mid-bite. We settled him in his pushchair, cake still in hand, and he woke an hour later and resumed eating as if he'd just been switched back on.

There was a temptation, and a bit of pressure, to invite neighbouring children to the party, or to cast around for all the people we know with kids of similar ages. But Oliver's too young for all that nonsense – we face years of strange smelling ugly kids trampling cake through our house and expecting a goody bag in return. I'm not going to hasten that nightmare, just because it's expected of us as loving parents.

It's my party and I'll cry...
Keeping a lid on birthdays

In all honesty the first birthday party should be filed under Competitive Dad Syndrome – if it wasn't for the fact that mums are just as guilty of over egging this particular celebratory pudding.

There's nothing wrong with throwing a huge party for your one year old, but don't pretend it's actually for the child's benefit. Your baby will probably sleep through half of it, dividing the remainder of the time between diffidence and terror. At 12 months a baby can certainly enjoy the company of other children, but it's yet to be scientifically verified that they enjoy pass the parcel.

The first birthday party is all about projection – you're happy that your parenting skills have negotiated your child to this landmark, and you want to show that off to the world. Fine, but don't plan a huge extravaganza if you aren't prepared for your child to get bored within five minutes, or throw up at an inopportune moment.

Don't let it become a matter of enormous stress, involving outside catering and portable loos. No-one will think any worse of you as a father and your child won't remember a thing in any case. It's good sense to ask someone to record the highlights of the party on video – especially if you're missing key events while running around topping up drinks and serving food. Don't be tempted to shoot the video yourself, or you'll miss even more of the party.

Anyway, how many kids get a holiday to Ireland as a birthday present? Not many, I'll wager – because not many parents are foolish enough to take their cake stuffed children on rough sea voyages way past their bedtime.

But that's exactly what we're doing. Oliver had a bit of a tantrum in the car, and he's been virtually impossible to settle in our 'deluxe' cabin right over the bow doors. One of the ship's PA speakers is just outside the cabin door, booming out rolling adverts for the cinema and Paddy O'Themepub's good time bar.

Lindsay is resigned to another long night and has agreed to sleep with Oliver in her bunk. I can't sleep at all, so I wandered the corridors of the ship, stopped at Paddy's for a quick pint, then returned to the cabin to read in my bunk.

It's 11.04pm. I've been looking at my watch for the last five minutes, waiting for the hands to inch round. Exactly one year ago this minute, my son was introduced to the world. I've been trying to remember exactly how I felt back then. The boat is rocking, and the beer has made me dizzy. My stomach lurches and I'm severely short of sleep. Yep, that was it. Fatherhood in a nutshell – everything is different and nothing changes. What a ride.

Epilogue

Let the record show that Oliver Giles took his first tentative steps on a beautiful, deserted beach in County Kerry. He took to the idea almost immediately and by the time we were back from Ireland he was starting to make a break for independence.

I don't know whether the strange rollercoaster of Oliver's first year has had any adverse impact on his development. The changes in principal carer might have been a bad thing, but it's helped him get used to both our styles of parenting, and it means we're an interchangeable unit. He calls us both 'mum'. I'm proud of that, pleased to say that I can spend quality time with my son without it being a terrific stress. I still try to take him to bookshops and on cultural trips. He still rebels.

While we continue to explore ways to improve the work/life balance, we do feel we've got the balance of care just about right. We always aimed at 50-50 childcare and right now it's about 60-40, with Lindsay taking the larger share. When she's back working again, the balance will shift once more, but neither of us plans to be a full time carer again.

In other ways our family life has taken on a peculiarly traditional edge. Oliver comes to me for play, to his mother for hugs and comfort. Now he's mobile, he loves to race around the neighbourhood and I can't resist the temptation to show him off all over again. He has an entire cupboard filled with footballs I've bought him to practice with.

I'm projecting more than just my sporting hopes onto the boy. He's become such a sponge for information, soaking up new words and noises. I have to be very careful about the words I choose around him – especially those which I apply to certain members of the family. I know that one day this charming game of parrots will bite me on the arse.

Until then, I'm just enjoying the experience of having a playmate that I can be unashamedly stupid with. We devise ridiculous games, we try to trump each other with the volume of our 'raspberry' fart noises and we mess around at the table.

The latter has been a cause of some concern in the house. As Oliver moves from a milk based diet to more solids, he needs to start learning some table manners – not easy with me gurning at him all the time. Lindsay has to play the grown-up to get us both to eat properly. I know it's not fair, I know it undermines a vital element of her parenting, but it also demonstrates a vital part of mine – it's great to have someone around who thinks you're a genius for making fart sounds.

Joined-up parenting is tough to implement, but I do appreciate how unfair it is that I'm constantly undermining Lindsay's attempts to impose rules and limits on Oliver's behaviour. It's also very confusing for the boy.

Dads are the usual culprits when it comes to this kind of misbehaviour because we generally have limited time with our children and want it to be as enjoyable as possible. Don't want your dinner? Have a biscuit instead. Result, I'm a hero for a few minutes and Lindsay's carefully designed nutrition plan goes out the window. It's neither fair nor constructive and it won't actually help me in the long run – I'll just end up with a son who's an expert in playing me off against his mother.

In the six months since his first birthday, he's gone from being a baby to a proper, fully fledged boy. He's become an individual who still has his fair share of tantrums, bumps and bruises, but who is also putting words and thoughts together, making connections and understanding the world around him.

With me as a father it's incredible that he's as amazing as he is today. But I can only appreciate just how amazing he is because I made sure I was there for the whole journey – I was even in the driving seat for some of it.

My first year of fatherhood wasn't about dominating the nappy changes, or proving I could be Lindsay's equal as a mother – it wasn't even just about having fun – it was about settling comfortably into a relationship with my son, and realising how far it could take me.

Looking back over this first year, I'm surprised at how I've turned out as a dad – more anxious, more hands-on, more serious and responsible. It's been a voyage of self-discovery – but not one that's set in stone. I continue to analyse what I expected from fatherhood and whether I've met those expectations. In some ways I have, in other areas I desperately want to change.

I haven't enjoyed every aspect of this tough first year, but that doesn't put me off – there'll still be ups and downs but I know it's going to get easier and the rewards are going to be more tangible. I find it easier to talk to other dads without bullshitting now, especially since I embraced and managed my competitive edge – 'my name is Stephen and I have Competitive Dad Syndrome'.

•   •   •

Now that life is calming down another question has been doing the rounds at our place. Does Oliver need a sibling? Given our fondness for living in wild and uninhabitable parts of the country the answer ought to be a resounding yes – despite my protests, he does need playmates more his own age.

But there's a lot to consider – the impact on our relationship, on the relationship we're building with Oliver, and the fact that we'd need to buy one of those crappy people movers if we ever want to go anywhere. Generally speaking, friends and relations seem to think we've been lucky with Oliver. He is certainly a good boy, maybe another baby would be a nightmare – demonstrating to the whole world that Oliver's exceptional behaviour is just a fluke and we are, in fact, terrible parents.

Most of all, I wonder whether I'd be prepared for another nine months of living like a spare part, dealing with all the medical personnel and then going through the sleepless nights and impotent fears of early fatherhood.

The answer's simple – having another baby would count as certifiable madness. But then again…

Conclusion
Mastering the art – six goals for a great dad

Let's go back to the beginning – the art of being a great dad. The wisdom of all the fathers who have contributed to this book has helped me in my own efforts to improve as a dad and creates a pretty solid foundation for any new father looking to do his best. There will be things that work for you and things that don't, especially as we all have such unique experiences. But I believe there are six goals that will provide a good start for any and every new dad.

Be there – there's no knowledge without experience, so get stuck in and not just for the good stuff – tackling baths, feeding, nappies and tantrums will bring you closer to your child.

Be consistent – don't undermine your partner, even if it scores you points with the baby. Presenting a united front as parents helps your baby learn and it'll probably save your relationship.

Be cool – give your child the space to develop a distinct personality and try not to project too many of your own hopes and dreams.

Be flexible – don't stick to a regime for its own sake and don't feel obliged to accept the advice of people who have 'been there, done that'.

Be aware – your role isn't just about relationship building with your child, it's about maintaining existing relationships with your partner, family and friends.

Be confident – fatherhood creates an increased sense of purpose and security. The more you master as a father, the more confident and relaxed you'll become in the role.

Contact us

You're welcome to contact White Ladder Press if you have any questions or comments for either us or the author. Please use whichever of the following routes suits you.

Phone: 01803 813343 between 9am and 5.30pm

Email: enquiries@whiteladderpress.com

Fax: 01803 813928

Address: White Ladder Press, Great Ambrook, Near Ipplepen, Devon TQ12 5UL

Website: **www.whiteladderpress.com**

What can our website do for you?

If you want more information about any of our books, you'll find it at **www.whiteladderpress.com**. In particular you'll find extracts from each of our books, and reviews of those that are already published. We also run special offers on future titles if you order online before publication. And you can request a copy of our free catalogue.

Many of our books also have links pages, useful addresses and so on relevant to the subject of the book. You'll also find out a bit more about us and, if you're a writer yourself, you'll find our submission guidelines for authors. So please check us out and let us know if you have any comments, questions or suggestions.

Fancy another good read?

If you've enjoyed this book, how about reading Stephen Giles's earlier book for fathers? If your baby hasn't been born yet – or if you'd simply like to relive those nine months of pregnancy – try *From Lad to Dad How to survive as a pregnant father*.

Just as in *You're the Daddy*, Stephen takes a father's perspective as he shares his ignorance, humiliations, frustrations, inadequacies and downright sodding terror. He holds your hand through all those new discoveries, from midwives and hospital visits to scary mood swings (hers as well as yours) and the looming prospect of having to reinvent yourself as a halfway decent dad.

He also passes on the answers to many of his own questions, along with a mass of practical and realistic advice, and reassures you that if he can survive as a pregnant father, so can you. In fact not only can you survive, but you can emerge at the end of it all feeling bloody fantastic.

Over the page is an extract from *From Lad to Dad*. If you like the look of it and want to order a copy you can use the order form at the back of the book, call us on 01803 813343 or order online at **www.whiteladderpress.com**.

Stephen Giles descibes the fears and frustrations of impending fatherhood with honesty and humour, along with practical help and advice.

Lawrence Dallaglio

From Lad to Dad

Extract

from Chapter Four
Long Hot Summer

I am so glad that Lindsay is back from her course. Not just because it means I can stop feeling pressured to do something meaningless and wild in her absence, but because I worry about her every movement. I spend so much time imagining possible problems and traumas that it becomes a great relief to see her fit and well at the end of each day.

And she is well. Not only that, she is blooming. She's decided that she'll take some holiday then start maternity leave early, essentially giving up work at 30 weeks. It's a relief for me, but a bigger one for her – her loyalties have been split between wanting to do a good job and wanting to get on with the whole baby thing.

She gets a pile of e-mails every day from eager baby product manufacturers, trying to impart knowledge and shift a few nappies into the bargain. Each of these has general tips for well-being and a few pointers on what to look out for. My favourite one arrived this morning. It said something along the lines of 'don't be disturbed if your partner starts to behave differently. He may take up a hobby, like woodwork, or grow a moustache'. Come on, you people, how many men have actually responded to the news of impending fatherhood by growing facial hair? And woodwork?

"Darling, I'm pregnant."

"That's wonderful darling. And look, I've made a pipe rack."

"You animal. Come here, I want to feel your stubble against my cheek."

I appreciate the general message that is coming across here – men tend to act more grown-up in response to the approaching demands of fatherhood. Most blokes I know feel they aren't ready for the new arrival, that they still have plenty of growing up to do themselves. That's absolutely understandable and totally human. But woodwork? Moustaches? God no, please don't let it be true.

I should add at this stage that my incredulity bears no relation to the fact that I was kicked out of woodwork at school and have always been cursed with a thin beard. It's just grade A bullshit, pure and simple.

"And we call this a nappy..."
Dealing with stereotypes

It might be bullshit, but it is a symptom of a wider problem that you've probably already started to encounter, and will certainly come up against as the due date approaches. You are about to be stereotyped, bracketed, patronised and condescended to on a scale not seen since you had that maths teacher with B.O. in the third year. It'll come from everywhere – from parents who've done it all, from medical professionals, from books and from TV.

You are a buffoon, a gibbering idiot who forgets to pack the bag, gets lost in the hospital, puts on nappies back to front, passes out in the delivery suite etc, etc. Think of every cliché and comic image of fathers-to-be, and you'll be labelled with almost all in the next couple of months. Is this a bad thing? It depends on your reaction. If it angers you, then it's bad. If you start to believe it, that's a tragedy. But low expectations could give you the space you need to get confident about your role before and after the birth. After all, if everyone's expecting you to fall flat on your face, every little success will feel great.

•　•　•

For the last few weeks Lindsay has been feeling serious movements from the baby. They started about six weeks ago as a fluttering sensation and have been building in intensity ever since. While it was still a novelty, she'd shout to me to come and feel her belly. By the time I got there, the baby was done stretching and had settled back to sleep, or it had shifted sufficiently to start booting her lower spine instead.

Only recently have the kicks been so powerful and frequent that I've been able to feel them too. It's such a weird feeling, and so hard to visualise the little foot or elbow that's stretching Lindsay's skin and fighting for a bit more room inside. In one sense it's great to be able to feel and see the growth of the child, but in another way it also reinforces the fact that I'm just an observer of this curious double act.

Lindsay's even started to detect a pattern of waking and sleeping at fixed times. The baby's most awake at about 3am, but I'm hoping it'll grow out of it. I'm a little jealous of the unmistakeable and unavoidable closeness that's building up between my wife and child.

The other disadvantage of a regular pattern of kicks and punches is that I fly into an immediate panic if Lindsay says the baby has gone quiet. I really should have invested in that portable ultrasound monitor – I bet I could have picked one up on E-Bay.

This happened just yesterday. Lindsay went off to work like normal, but through breakfast, she'd been worried about the fact that she hadn't felt the baby move for a few hours. I wanted her to stay at home, maybe go into the hospital for a scan, but we looked at the books again and they seemed to suggest it wasn't always something to worry about. After about 28 weeks, it ought to be normal to detect around 10 distinct movements every day, but until then the odd lengthy period without a flinch isn't a big worry.

Unfortunately, the downside of working from home is that you've got nothing to distract you from worrying that there is a real problem. With mother and child half an hour away at work, all I could do was sit and fret. Well, that was my excuse for playing computer games all day.

Is there anybody there?
Getting help and guidance

Assuming that you want to avoid being talked down to by smug new fathers – who a few short months ago were crapping themselves in your shoes (as it were) – your options for expressing and discussing your fears are limited. While it's good to talk to your partner, you might want to verify the facts a bit before you involve and worry her about something that turns out to be totally irrelevant. Your fears might also be about her, of course. Childless mates won't be a lot of use, so the only real hope lies in other fathers-to-be.

The question is, how do you get access to them? Some may attend antenatal classes (more of which later) but these are often taken late on in the pregnancy. There are a few message boards online for dads only, but a glance through some of the more popular boards suggests that they are frequently invaded by mums-to-be, so they aren't generally too open and frank.

The truth – and the reason for this book's existence – is that true empathy is hard to find. I was lucky enough to have a couple of mates going through the process around the same time as me, but even then I didn't share experiences with them as often as I could, and should, have done. The fact is that you will get through by relying on a variety of different sources – an informative web site, a good book, a decent friend, an understanding partner. They can all help, but not one of them can give you all the answers.

Of course, Lindsay came home and reported that she'd gone 12 rounds with the little thug during a vital business meeting and I breathed a sigh of relief. I really, really should get out more.

Babies
for Beginners

If it isn't in here,
you don't need to know it.

At last, here is the book for every new parent who's never been quite sure what a cradle cap is and whether you need one. **Babies for Beginners** cuts the crap — the unnecessary equipment, the overfussy advice — and gives you the absolute basics of babycare: keep the baby alive, at all costs, and try to stop it getting too hungry.

From bedtime to bathtime, mealtime to playtime, this book highlights the CORE OBJECTIVE of each exercise (for example, get the baby bathed) and the KEY FOCUS (don't drown it). By exploding the myths around each aspect of babycare, the book explains what is necessary and what is a bonus; what equipment is essential and what you can do without.

Babies for Beginners is the perfect book for every first time mother who's confused by all the advice and can't believe it's really necessary to spend that much money. And it's the ultimate guide for every father looking for an excuse to get out of ante-natal classes.

Roni Jay is a professional author whose books include **KIDS & Co: winning business tactics for every family**. She is the mother of three young children, and stepmother to another three grown up ones.

£7.99

Full Time Father

HOW TO SUCCEED AS A STAY AT HOME DAD

"At last, a hands-on, amusing and above all realistic guide for dads who have given up work to bring up their children. What makes this book so rewarding is that it is written by a father who has been there, seen it and done it."
Nick Cavender, Chairman, HomeDad UK

So your partner earns more than you do?
You've been made redundant? You hate the job?
Being a full time dad can make a lot of sense.

But isn't it a bit weird? Actually no; it's a growing trend. Nearly one in ten fathers in the UK now takes the main responsibility for looking after the kids, often full time.

It's a big decision though. What will your mates think? Will you ever get a decent job again? Won't you miss the cut and thrust of the office? And won't you go stark staring mad without any mental stimulation too sophisticated for a toddler? It's not just you, either. It's the whole family set up. Who wears the trousers? Who controls the family purse? And does it mean you have to clean the house and do the shopping, too?

Full Time Father is written by a stay at home dad and draws on his survey of other 'homedads' as well as on his own experience. It examines all the key issues, passes on masses of valuable tips and advice, and lets the reader know what to expect – both good and bad – should they decide to become a homedad themselves.

£9.99

Order form

You can order any of our books via any of the contact routes on page 106, including on our website. Or fill out the order form below and fax it or post it to us.

We'll normally send your copy out by first class post within 24 hours (but please allow five days for delivery). We don't charge postage and packing within the UK. Please add £1 per book for postage outside the UK.

Title (Mr/Mrs/Miss/Ms/Dr/Lord etc)

Name

Address

Postcode

Daytime phone number

Email

No. of copies	Title	Price	Total £
Postage and packing £1 per book (outside the UK only):			
	TOTAL:		

Please either send us a cheque made out to White Ladder Press Ltd or fill in the credit card details below.

Type of card ☐ Visa ☐ Mastercard ☐ Switch

Card number

Start date (if on card) _____ Expiry date _____ Issue no (Switch) _____

Name as shown on card

Signature